Secrets about Guys

[that shouldn't be secret]

Grace Dove

Cover and interior design by Ahaa! Design
Cover and interior photos by Austin Bewsey Studios
Edited by Dale Reeves and Lynn Lusby Pratt

Library of Congress Cataloging-in-Publication Data:
Dove, Grace, 1945-
    Secrets about guys : (that shouldn't be secret) / Grace Dove.
        p. cm.
    ISBN 0-7847-1544-0 (soft cover)
1. Teenage boys. 2. Young men. 3. Interpersonal relations in adolescence. 4. Interpersonal
relations—Religious aspects—Christianity. 5. Man-woman relationships—Religious aspects—
Christianity. I. Title.
HQ797.D68 2005
241'.6765—dc22

2005002691

Published in association with the literary agency of Alive Communications, Inc.,
7680 Goddard St., Suite 200, Colorado Springs, Colorado 80920.

Standard Publishing, Cincinnati, Ohio.
A division of Standex International Corporation.

12 11 10 09 08 07 06   7 6 5 4 3 2

ISBN: 0-7847-1544-0

Secrets about Guys

[that shouldn't be secret]

Grace Dove

refuge™

an imprint of
Standard Publishing
www.rfgbooks.com

For my husband, Kevin,
and our three sons, Aaron, Andrew and Luke.
You are my heroes.

Contents

Acknowledgments

Many precious people had a part in this book; sometimes they didn't even know it, but God surely used them. With deepest appreciation I want to thank . . .

• Donna Dickey for revealing the deep longing young women today have to learn about guys and homemaking. And Abbie, Jill, Katie, Kristina, Laura, Leila, Melissa, Rachel and Stevie for confirming this interest.

• Annelise and Alana, two very special princesses.

• Jacquelynn Thompson Orme. God sent you at just the right time.

• Mike Crow, Ph.D., my friend and hero in the faith, who prayed.

• Nathan Unseth, my brother-in-the-Lord, who both encourages me and helps me stay real.

• Dr. James Dobson, whose Focus on the Family video series laid valuable foundations for our parenting even before our first son was born.

• My parents who are now part of the "great cloud of witnesses." Mom, you were my role model for learning to be a godly wife and mother. And Dad, who never withheld forgiveness when I needed it.

• Marilyn Dove, my stepmother-in-law and a much-published writer who generously mentored and encouraged me—for years! And my father-in-law, Clem Dove; I love you both.

• Chris Thompson, my steadfast friend who prayed me through every step of this book. Your optimism and enthusiasm are contagious!

• Colleen Bowers, my kindred-spirit friend and fellow author. The

Lord knows I couldn't have done this without you! I really mean it. Now finish *your* book!

• My other two prayer partners, Gina Cobb, my sister-in-the-Lord, and Ione Mansfield, my real-life sister.

• Nancy and Ann, also my real-life sisters with whom I delight in being a female. I am so blessed.

• My four brothers, Dale, Alan, John and Phil, all whom I admire tremendously.

• Marty Kasza, I so admire your kindness and humility.

• Huge hugs for God's angel, Susie Shellenberger, editor of *Brio,* who delivered his message confirming I was to write this book. You have changed my life. You are truly "Jesus with skin on."

• Tons of thanks to my agent, Andrea Christian, at Alive Communications. Your patience, encouragement, enthusiasm, expertise and faith in me are a gift beyond measure.

• Dale Reeves at Standard Publishing, thank you for sharing my vision for this book and for making it happen.

• Lynn Lusby Pratt, copy editor at Standard, you're amazing!

• And to my heavenly Father, on whom I am so dependent, I give my deepest thanks. Your mercy truly endures forever.

"Anything will give up its secrets
if you love it enough."

—George Washington Carver

Introduction

Pssst!

Wanna Know a Secret?

When it comes to guys, what we females don't know *can* hurt us—and *them!*

It might shock you to learn how much you're affected by what you don't know about guys. Girls tend to take guys too much at face value. When we do that, it's easy to unknowingly sabotage a potential friendship with them before it has time to develop. The truth is, there's a whole lot more to guys than we see on the surface. Guys are wonderfully complex. They have a ton of secrets that shouldn't be secret!

In all honesty, guys *want* you to know these things. It isn't that they're trying to keep secrets, but it's not information that they are willing—or dare—to tell you. Hey, guys dig girls and don't want to offend them.

Sometimes, it simply doesn't occur to them to talk about these issues with girls. Guys admit they don't even tell their own sisters this stuff—though girls need to know—and guys *wish* girls knew it. Hmmm, it looks like we have a dilemma here, right?

Not anymore. This book is loaded with their secrets. And how did I find them out? I've been surrounded by guys most of my life. I grew up with four brothers, and lived to tell about it. (I also have three sisters, which is why I survived.)

Now that I'm married, I still have four guys in my life—a fabulous hubby and three cool sons. Between them and their friends, I've been hostess to a multitude of guys for over twenty years. Needless to say, living in a guy's world has meant a lot to me. (For one thing, it means the toilet seat is never down.)

But what it *really* means is that I've discovered a lot of guys' secrets! Not just from the guys in our home but from lots of other guys too. I've interviewed dozens of them, even talked to young men right off the street (with my husband's approval). And the guys have wholeheartedly given me the green light to share their secrets with you!

Not only are these secrets no longer going to be secret, but guys earnestly want you to find all this out. What more could we ask?

Guys have their own way of thinking, which isn't the way we females think. That's what this book is about—learning what guys *really* think . . . *how* they think . . . *why* they think it . . . how that influences what they *do*—and how it all affects you. So keep reading, because the guys are really hoping you will!

Secret No. 1

Guys Appreciate Modesty

They don't like the temptations. But guys are often part of the problem because they *do* give attention to provocatively dressed girls. And girls misinterpret that attention. Girls are confused by today's fashion trends as well. Though extremely revealing clothing has been in vogue only a short time, it's been long enough that today's teen girls have grown up with these styles and see them as normal. So who has the right to say what's modest anyway? That's where the Bible comes in. It shows that God's standards fit every culture and every era—and he *enjoys* adorning his people!

[Sure, it's hard to believe that guys prefer modesty. Every day we're bombarded with messages that scream just the opposite.]

Movies, television shows, advertising, magazines and definitely the mall—all tell us that being scantily clad is *the* way to catch a guy.

It's no secret that girls wearing skimpy outfits attract guys' attention. That's why the media uses alluring models for advertising. It works! It does get guys' attention! It catches our attention too, doesn't it? We see the guys looking and automatically buy into the notion that uncovering our bodies is what guys want us to do to attract them. But have we ever asked them?

Since God created guys to be visually stimulated, they can't help but notice girls who expose their bodies. But there's a wide gap between guys who glance at a provocatively dressed girl and guys who actually choose a girl like that for a wife.

One guy explained the difference like this: "There's a certain level of attraction, but if you're interested in a girl for the long term, not just for dating, you're looking for someone who is attractive but not showing off too much."

Now, at first that might not seem fair. Why would guys separate girls into two categories: "dating only" or "potential wives"? But really, what else can guys do? By the way they dress, girls communicate which group they fit into, and guys just respond accordingly. Is it any more fair for a girl to dress seductively, only to insist that she's "not that kind of girl"?

It would be ridiculous to say that no guys choose females who dress that way. Of course some do. But girls who attract guys by using their bodies need to remember a couple of things. First of all . . .

> If physical attraction is your sole bait for
> luring a guy, you'll only feel secure with him
> as long as you look provocative.

Isn't that a stressful and fearful way to try hanging onto a relationship? It's also terribly unrealistic. Lots of situations can change or control your appearance. For example, after you're married, what happens when you become pregnant and your curves move to new locations? Or, worse yet, when he sees you *after* you've given birth! Trust me; you're not gonna want to wear form-fitting clothing then!

Those are normal events of life. And there are others. What about how you look (and smell) first thing in the morning? Eeeuw. Or when you're sick, or you gain a few pounds, or get a zit or a bad haircut or . . . ? There are reasons girls aren't portrayed in those realistic everyday situations by advertisers trying to sell products!

Less predictable events in life also can affect a relationship that is based solely on physical attraction. What happens if circumstances such as camp, school, military service, jobs or other commitments separate you from your guy for a while? Will he stay true to you? If he's snared by your body, how can you be sure that his affections won't go elsewhere when someone comes along who looks more enticing?

We're going to take a deeper look at this in the next chapter, but this is too exciting to wait until then to tell you:

> Though guys are easily attracted
> by your appearance, they are
> majorly attracted by your personality.

You can change only so much about your outward appearance—and your looks *will* change with time—but your personality and character can continuously become more beautiful for the rest of your life! Since guys are captivated by an engaging personality, you can have a lot goin' for you if you work on that.

Besides, do you *really* want to depend solely on your looks to catch and keep a guy? And do you really *want* a guy who only cares about how you look? He doesn't sound like much of a knight in shining armor, does he?

That brings up the second point. Girls who use the show-off-your-body method for catching a guy also need to remember that the quality of the guy she attracts will be determined by the way he is attracted to her. That is super important!

Generally speaking, "like attracts like." If you want a truly godly guy, you must cultivate becoming a truly godly woman. For example, say your wish list for what you want in a guy goes something like this: has a great personality, is trustworthy, friendly, fun, caring and has goals for a successful future. (I know I skipped really cute. That goes without saying!) This list contains clues for what traits need to be developed in *you*. Your kind of dream guy isn't going to be spending his time ogling girls. Sure, he'll notice them. We already talked about that. But the girl that catches his eye—and keeps his heart—will be a young lady who reflects his values!

Even if you do have some similar values, if you're wearing revealing clothing, that special guy will probably never discover them because he won't stick around long enough to find out.

[
A guy's first impression of a girl comes from the way she's dressed.
]

(The second is in a later chapter!)

Your grooming sends a nonverbal message. Have you ever noticed that you're treated differently in public depending upon your attire? Not just by guys. The level of courtesy you receive from public servants, such as department store clerks, is often determined by the way you're dressed. What you wear makes a statement about what you think of yourself as well. When females dress seductively they *are* expressing what is in their hearts, even though they may not admit it to themselves.

It's tough not to be influenced by advertising when we're deciding what clothes to buy, what makeup to wear and what image we want to convey. But in most cases, ads don't represent guys' opinions. Remember, advertising is meant to convince you to buy products. Tight tops, extra-short skirts and clothes that show too much skin are actually intimidating to many young men and make them uncomfortable.

In a survey of teen guys in a youth group, an overwhelming majority stated that they wished girls would dress more modestly.

[
Eighty-six percent commented that girls wear tops
that are too revealing!
]

Two-thirds said that current styles of dresses, skirts and shorts are not modest enough. One section of the survey allowed the guys to add any comments they wanted. Because they could remain anonymous, the guys dared to share what they really thought. Here are some of their statements:

"God has blessed girls with beauty inside and out. It's not necessary for them to reveal their body—or portions of it—to entice."

"Put some clothes on!"

"It's not all about what you wear that we like—it's your heart and personality."

"I wish girls knew that dressing immodestly is really a stumbling block for guys."

"Please dress modestly. Some girls wear extremely tight clothes and it actually turns guys off. We want girls to be women of God, not lust magnets!"

"I wish women would try to attract men with their godly character, integrity and class, not just with their looks."

Kinda shocking, isn't it? That's just a little peek into what guys really think. Remember, those are *their* words! Rarely, if ever, will guys openly offer this information. How can they? If you were a guy, would you dare to tell a girl, "Hey, would you mind wearing a longer skirt?" or "You know, I really don't appreciate seeing your cleavage."

I'm aware of a family that began looking for another church, partly because of the way a few girls in the youth group dressed. It was a stumbling block for their teenage son who was grieved by the temptations he faced, even in a worship service, because of the girls' immodesty.

That wasn't an isolated case. A conversation between a Bible school student and my husband was very sobering. This young man confided his anger after attending a party where church and other Bible school students were gathered in a home. He was shocked by the revealing clothing worn by the girls, and frustrated that he had to face those enticements. He told my husband something like, "I know they've got curves but do they have to show every detail?"

[
Sometimes, you are showing details
you may not intend!
]

While looking in the mirror at home, you may think you're dressed adequately. But if your top is snug and your bra is made of a thin fabric, and it's cold—you may be showing much more than you realize! The most embarrassing thing is, well, it's sort of like having a bit of broccoli in your teeth—no one is going to tell you! When guys see your "details," they react in different ways: some blush, some will leer and make jokes with their buddies and some, like the young man above, become angry.

And who can blame them? In daily life, guys are blatantly confronted with female nudity on billboards, magazine and newspaper racks and TV commercials. Even when they want to, they can't avoid it. So when guys are in a church-related setting, they expect it to be a safe place where they will find relief from the lewdness in the world. It's no wonder that young man was outraged when even among church friends he couldn't escape from those kinds of temptations.

The clothing of today's young ladies can be even more difficult for married men to deal with. A married man knows what's under the clothing. He has experienced the pleasures of a wife. Therefore, *much* less is left to the imagination when a young lady is around. A group of married men took a survey similar to the one the youth group guys filled out and the results verified this.

Ninety-three percent said they were not totally comfortable with the way girls and women currently dress. Ninety-eight percent said they have been distracted by a girl's or woman's appearance in a church service! That's almost every man! (Your mother might want to know this too.)

One married man wrote this comment on the survey: "If you want to enhance your femininity, don't display your body. The attention you get from exposure is not honoring God or yourselves. If a man of honor must turn his head because of what you are wearing, what type of man are you attracting?"

Doesn't it seem sad to realize what a struggle our appearance can create for guys? Whose problem is this? Is it ours for the way we dress, or do the men just need to learn to stop being so "lustful"?

If you check a dictionary, you'll see that a general definition of the word *lust* is "an overwhelming desire." There is a difference between that and a man's instinctive reaction to seeing an immodestly dressed lady. Not every guy who reacts is lusting. But do you want to be a source of inciting either response? Jesus has some strong words about that.

"How terrible it will be for anyone who causes others to sin. Temptation to do wrong is inevitable, but how terrible it will be for the person who does the tempting" (Matthew 18:7, NLT).

[
It's clear the Lord is telling us that we are held responsible for knowingly being a source of stumbling in someone else's life.
]

We also see this in Genesis 3. God held the serpent responsible for tempting Eve and Eve responsible for tempting Adam. We don't want God's "woe" on us, do we, ladies?

Since I'm the mother of three sons, I tend to see things through their eyes, but I'm also a female and I *do* remember what it is like to be a single young lady. I understand wanting to feel attractive, pretty, trendy, fashionable and imaginative. It's fun! During all the years I was growing up, my goal was to be a fashion designer and illustrator. I sewed my own clothes and wanted to create beautiful styles for women. Today, I still enjoy pretty and creative clothing tremendously.

Probably every woman understands the temptation to dress provocatively. It's flattering, even exhilarating, to have people look at you, and it certainly feeds the female ego to have guys notice. But dressing seductively to satisfy that desire for attention harms everyone involved.

So what's the solution? *How are we supposed to dress? Do we have to look frumpy just to avoid being a stumbling block? I feel angry. Do I have to throw out my wardrobe? I love looking pretty! Can't I enjoy clothes anymore?*

Are those some of your thoughts? The subject of modesty can be touchy because it might seem subjective, like opinions differ, right?

Sure they do, and I'm not the fashion police either. When I give talks on modesty, I tell girls that I'm not trying to convince them to dress like me. They don't need to. One of the wonderful things about knowing God is discovering that he has planted in everyone a measure of creativity. There's room for a wide array of imaginative styles that please the Lord. He is the one who designed our bodies! If we check with him, we can find not only his guidelines for modesty that are solid and unwavering, but we also can tap into the Lord's endless source of creative ideas! There's nothing wrong with fashions and trends changing. God likes variety too!

But there *is* a problem when standards of morality decline. In searching the Scriptures to see what God has to say about the proper way for women to dress, I came upon some thought-provoking information *and* some very exciting surprises!

Did you know that throughout most of history, prostitutes were identifiable by the way they dressed? Even back in Bible days. Proverbs 7:10 says, "Then out came a woman to meet him, dressed like a prostitute and with crafty intent." (See also Genesis 38:15.) This identity-by-apparel was true even as recently as when your grandmother was a girl. She could probably tell you that those "ladies of the night" were easily spotted on the streets by their scanty, tight-fitting tops and their skin-tight pants or skirts.

Can we identify prostitutes in our society today by that standard? Probably not. What has changed? Have prostitutes and immoral women started dressing more modestly so that they blend into mainstream society? Sadly, we have to admit that it's just the opposite.

> In the past few years, the decline in morality
> has spiraled downward so rapidly that, for the
> first time in history, the attire of prostitutes
> has become the fashion of the day.

Though these extremely revealing styles are a fairly recent development, they have been around long enough that today's young ladies have grown up with them. That's why the look is so easy for girls to accept as normal. Pop stars, actresses and models commonly set the trends. Young ladies look to them as role models and want to look just like them. The problem is, the morals of most of today's celebrities have been thrown aside, and without giving it much thought, girls are embracing that same standard (Psalm 106:35, 36).

How can we avoid getting caught in the moral decay? When trying to dress modestly, or even judging the way we dress, we can't compare ourselves to other people. The only safe place to find solid guidelines is from the Lord.

> God's standards fit every culture and every era.
> Even the twenty-first century. God's ways work!

He explains his ways in his Word, the Bible. He tells us what doesn't work, what isn't acceptable, but also what pleases him.

When we compare many of the most popular styles today with the

Word of God, we see that they are not normal in God's eyes. They are indecent. But when we look into the Bible, we can also discover that it's possible to dress modestly *and* dress beautifully!

God is definitely a romantic. The Bible shows that he delights in the beauty of an intimate husband and wife relationship, not only in single verses (of which there are many; Hebrews 13:4, for example) but also in large portions of Scripture such as The Song of Songs. There's no shame connected with the romance and intimacy between a husband and wife. In marriage, the sweetness of flirtation has God's blessing. And our heavenly Father is very protective of the covenant of marriage.

It's important for us to understand and not lose sight of the Lord's attitude about marriage because other Bible references that refer to an uncovered or exposed body associate this condition with sin, shame, degradation (see Exodus 32:25-27, KJV; Ezekiel 23:18), judgment, punishment (see Isaiah 20:4; 47:1-3; Ezekiel 23:26; Hosea 2:3; Nahum 3:5) or poverty (see James 2:15, KJV)! The idolatry and nakedness of the people was no small matter to the Lord. God does not change. His views of idolatry and nakedness are still the same today.

The term *naked* does not necessarily mean having no clothing on at all. It also means scantily clad, not being covered adequately (Matthew 25:35-38, 44, KJV). God's attitude is so clear. It grieves him when his people are uncovered.

Don't beat yourself up if you are discovering that your views of modesty don't match God's. Even Adam and Eve didn't get it right the first time. After they sinned, they sewed leaves together to cover themselves (Genesis 3:7). God didn't see that as adequate because he provided different coverings for them (Genesis 3:21). God knew something about the significance of being properly clothed that Adam and Eve didn't understand. Now that we have the Bible, though, we don't have to make the same mistake.

> To the Lord, being adequately covered is a sign of his protection, favor and blessing.

It is also a sign of being under God's authority. If people in the world could see how dearly God loves them, they wouldn't shrink from his mandates. Being properly adorned isn't a burden. It's a status symbol; it indicates that we're part of his kingdom!

What are girls and women today saying when they expose so much of their bodies? Without realizing it, are women rejecting God's authority and stepping out of his protective covering?

Because young ladies today have grown up with these scanty styles, some of them may not understand how provocatively they're dressing. A fifteen-year-old girl e-mailed me, insisting that girls know *exactly* what they're doing when they dress that way! (And plenty of guys certainly insist girls know. A guy can look a girl squarely in the eye and have a conversation with her, never revealing the offense he feels inside because of the immodest way she's dressed.) Either way, the Lord knows your heart; he sees everything in your life and he cares deeply. You're a treasure to him; God wants you protected, blessed and covered!

God likes to not only cover his people but also lavishly adorn them! He goes far beyond being neutral or merely tolerant of our apparel. Ezekiel 16:8, 10-13 is a beautiful example. "I spread the corner of my garment over you and covered your nakedness. . . . I clothed you with an embroidered dress and put leather sandals on you. I dressed you in fine linen and covered you with costly garments. I adorned you with jewelry: I put bracelets on your arms and a necklace around your neck, and I put a ring on your nose, earrings on your ears and a beautiful crown on your head. So you were adorned with gold and silver; your clothes were of fine linen and costly fabric and embroidered cloth."

Doesn't he sound like a generous Father? Here, the Lord was speaking of Jerusalem. In the context of that chapter, Jerusalem spoiled the blessing by becoming vain, proud and lewd. But that doesn't negate God's desire to bless his people. We see this same attitude of generosity in the New Testament as well, in the story of the prodigal son. The father ran to meet him and immediately wanted to adorn his son with the best of everything (Luke 15:20, 22).

Now, am I saying to use this information as an excuse to go on a spending spree at the mall? Ummm, no. Of course not. In these examples, the Lord initiated the adorning. He pursued giving the blessing; the recipients didn't race after it. But it's important to understand how lovingly the Lord looks upon you and delights in blessing his children. He's not against your looking attractive. A key here is in understanding that your true beauty comes from within, and that is what you should concentrate on first (1 Timothy 2:9, 10; 1 Peter 3:3-5).

> If you feel that you need to make some adjustments in your wardrobe, why not ask the Lord for ideas and help in bringing it into alignment with what pleases him?

Can you imagine how it will touch his heart to know that you want to obey him? Since you know it's his desire, you can be sure he will answer you (1 John 5:14, 15).

What a thrill! You might even want to get specific and tell him what colors you like! He's a very personal God. Can you see the adventure in this? Wow!

Mary was a missionary in northern Ontario, Canada. She traveled often and spent lots of time with people, so when she had the opportunity, she loved worshiping the Lord in the seclusion of her own room.

Mary was also single and depended heavily on the Lord for guidance and protection. While looking for reassurance one day, she read Psalm 91 and noticed verse 4: "He will cover you with his feathers, and under his wings you will find refuge." She understood about finding refuge in the Lord, but she couldn't help wondering what the "feathers" part was about. *Does God have feathers? Or is this just figurative language?* She made a note of the verse in her journal and forgot about it.

A few days later, a check from her brother arrived in the mail. He included a note explaining the money was for purchasing a winter parka so she would stay warm while traveling in the remote North Country.

Time passed before she was able to get her coat because it meant a trip to the big city to find such a jacket. But eventually she made it to the shop. At the recommendation of a knowledgeable coworker, she chose a red jacket; she'd be easier to spot in the snow if she got lost.

Back in her Ontario room, Mary decided to try it on again. Snuggling into the cozy goose-down jacket, the verse suddenly echoed in her memory. "He will cover you with his feathers." Mary began praising the Lord, laughing with delight at how literally he had done just that!

Oh, don't ever underestimate God's good pleasure when it comes to clothing you! Regarding fashion, who do we normally get our trends from?

> Doesn't it seem a little strange that Christians take their cues from the world?

The Lord wants to make his people "the head, not the tail" (Deuteronomy 28:13). We should be making our own fashion statements!

It's certainly understandable that young ladies don't want to dress like their mothers or grandmothers—they want their own look—but dressing young does not have to mean dressing scantily.

Instead of searching out the styles of the world and following those, virtuous young ladies can release their creativity and come up with fabulous, fresh new looks. It's possible, you know.

How is fashion created anyway? Stop and think about it. Whatever is in vogue comes about because someone decides to break away from the norm. Some individual exercises his or her imagination and comes up with a new idea. For example, when long, straight hair is stylish, it's because someone becomes tired of looking at curly hair and makes a change. Or vice versa. The person who designs hair to be short and curly has boldly decided to make a departure from the long, straight hair look of everyone else.

It takes courage to break away from the norm and do something different. There's always the risk of not being accepted. But our society admires, often idolizes, individuals who dare to be different and don't worry about what others think. Those creative and innovative people are the ones who originate new trends. Others see what they're doing and pay their highest compliments by copying them.

> Maybe God wants some fashion designers after his own heart! We have access to the ultimate creator, *the* master designer! He loves color, texture and variety.

Just look at his creation! With him, how can we possibly be lacking in creativity? Surely we can ask him to give us creative ideas that will enhance our appearance and glorify him. God knows it's possible to adorn his people both modestly and beautifully. Shouldn't we believe that too?

Proverbs 28:1 says the righteous are bold as a lion! That doesn't mean we should try to come up with outlandish fashion statements. But why not have the courage to set trends instead of following them?

Inspiration to design beautiful, modest attire needn't be with the motive of putting the world down or communicating rejection, but rather including them. Why not embrace the world with the message, "Look! It's possible to be creative and innovative without having to unnecessarily reveal our bodies." The goal is to *show* that our loving God and creator has a better way, and it includes everyone!

You are a new generation of young women. You have a fabulous opportunity to influence not only the guys in your lives but also the whole world with your nobility and virtue.

Guys wish that females would expose less of their bodies, but they're not likely to say it to girls. Since they're reflecting the heart of the Lord on this matter, perhaps they shouldn't have to say anything anyway. If we females just listen to the Lord, much of the battle that guys face would solve itself.

"The LORD does not look at the things man looks at. Man looks at the outward appearance, but the LORD looks at the heart" (1 Samuel 16:7).

[
Granted, the Lord looks on your heart,
but guys look on the outside!
]

At least they do at first. The closer a guy is to the Lord, the more he wants to see your heart, and the less he wants your outward appearance to be a distraction. Guys don't feel they can tell you that they want you to dress modestly, but they desperately wish girls knew. When you learn this one, you've discovered an extremely important secret. In all honesty, isn't it liberating to know that guys actually *prefer* modesty?

Let's see what *else* they prefer!

Secret No. 2

Guys Have Definite Ideas About Beauty

Beauty isn't everything. Not to guys anyway. It's true . . . really!

You don't believe me, do you? OK, I've heard my sons use words like *gorgeous* and *luscious* when describing girls. They tease, laugh and talk a LOT about attractive girls. But I've also heard them and their friends discuss very beautiful girls whom they have no desire to be around. So maybe the issue isn't whether or not beauty counts with guys, but rather what *they think* is beautiful.

We've already discovered that it isn't seductive dress. Guys have other secrets about what is (or isn't) beautiful to them too, and again, it isn't totally what the world says. It isn't completely centered on outward appearance either. Since there are beautiful girls whom guys aren't attracted to, there has to be a reason. Actually, there are numerous reasons.

Living in a world saturated with messages emphasizing the importance of how we look makes it difficult to believe that inner beauty matters—for everyone, not just teenagers. You've probably heard adults often discuss how much it means to young people to fit in with their crowd. But adults are really no different! They're just as inclined to want to fit in with their peer groups. Everyone falls prey to the same pressures—what to wear, how to look, what to own . . . it's all outward, visible stuff. It's difficult for anyone, regardless of age, to believe that inner beauty is more important.

> One reason so many people buy into the
> influence of outward appearance is because
> they don't understand that what we are
> inside shows on the outside!

Even for those who do understand, let's face it, it's much easier to change how we look outwardly than to develop inner character. That takes work! So even though developing one's personality enhances the inside *and* the outside, people spend most of their time trying to perfect themselves by concentrating on their outward appearance. Guys know this instinctively, if not consciously, and that's why they don't find all beautiful girls attractive.

Different guys have different ideas about what they find beautiful in a girl. Beauty definitely *is* in the eye of the beholder. Even my sons and their friends have varying opinions about who catches their eye and why. It's impossible to make a complete list of everything that wows guys because there are such a variety of males. Not all of them prefer big boobs, believe it or not! Some guys are attracted to a small waist or long legs, a girl's eyes, her lips, her hair . . . it's an endless list. I know of a man who was attracted to his future wife by how well her nails were manicured. Oh, but we're talking about inner beauty, aren't we? Well, maybe we should start with grooming then, even though that means we're still dealing with the exterior (in a way).

Good Grooming

Your outward appearance tells a great deal about your personality—your inner attitudes—how you feel about yourself and how you feel toward others. Being neat and clean sends a positive message that guys pick up on—and appreciate! Think of all that you're saying when you're well groomed:

I'm disciplined. (I made sure my clothes were clean and pressed.)

I'm thoughtful of others. (I showered so I'm fresh. And I didn't overload on fragrance!)

I'm grateful. (I appreciate my health and what I own, so I take care of it.)

I care about you. (Since I've prepared myself for the day, I don't have to feel self-conscious about my appearance; I'm free to think about others.)

I'm patient and self-controlled. (I made time for grooming and didn't throw myself together at the last minute.)

I like and respect myself. (I'm a valuable person who is worthy of receiving care and attention.)

In Secret No. 1, we learned the first thing that attracts a guy's attention is how a girl looks. The second thing a guy notices is her demeanor, how a girl acts. The way a girl is groomed directly affects how she conducts herself. Your inner self and your outward appearance are intrinsically linked. So, as well as speaking about your inner attitudes through your grooming, you are actually influencing your own behavior.

Think about the way you feel when you're dressed up for an event—perhaps a church service. You feel differently, don't you, after you've come home and changed out of your Sunday best into something more casual? Do you sit the same in either outfit? Walk the same? Most likely not. When wearing jeans at home you might flop down and fling a leg over an end of the sofa, but in a skirt? Probably not.

One easy way to improve your appearance, your manners and the way you conduct yourself is by giving care and attention to your grooming and to what you choose to wear. It won't stifle your personality but it can enhance it—make it shine—and that can bring out the "wow" from guys!

Let's get specific. What do guys think about girls' makeup, their hairstyles, nails, fragrances, etc.? From my observations and also what I hear, they actually enjoy it all—in moderation. One young man told me he genuinely likes when girls take time to fix themselves up.

If you want to know how guys feel about girls wearing fragrances, go ahead and ask. But don't try finding out by saying, "Hey, do you like this?" and then offering your wrist for him to sniff. That puts him on the spot, and he'll more likely try being diplomatic rather than truthful. But if you ask, "What do you think about girls wearing perfume?" then he might tell you—and he might even name a scent he especially likes. I asked a young man how he feels about girls wearing fragrances and he enthusiastically responded, "I think it's awesome!"

The key is moderation. A light spritz of eau de cologne is pleasing; overdone it's sickening. (Remember that if you wear the same scent all the time, you're going to be used to it, so without realizing it you may be applying more than you should.)

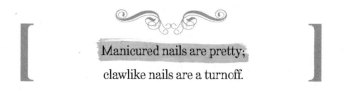

Manicured nails are pretty;
clawlike nails are a turnoff.

Mascara, foundation, lip, eye and cheek colors all can enhance your natural beauty, but if it's messy or overdone, guys are really repelled. When it comes to too much makeup being a turnoff, one guy said, "Underline that!" Another exclaimed, "Use less makeup!"

Melissa was a young lady who refused to ever be seen without makeup. She was extremely self-conscious and spent exorbitant amounts of time applying it. The truth was, she felt ugly. She hated herself and the way she looked. Wearing all that makeup was a mask to hide behind, and it was also her attempt at trying to make herself acceptable.

After Melissa became a Christian, her real personality started longing to emerge. She begged God to set her free from her addiction to makeup. At first, she stopped wearing it completely. People who were used to seeing Melissa all made up were shocked by the drastic change in her appearance, and that caused her to feel all the more self-conscious. As painful as that transition was, her longing to become real grew greater than her fear. She was excited by the freedom she began to experience by daring to be herself. In time Melissa learned not only to appreciate the unique appearance the Lord had given her but also how to apply makeup to highlight her special features.

Perhaps you know a girl who wears excessive amounts of makeup. Be kind. Don't judge. She may need a friend. You can't be certain of what's really in her heart until you get to know her.

If you find *yourself* imprisoned by makeup, take courage. Ask the Lord for help. He is just as willing to help you as he was the other young lady. He's your heavenly Father and you're precious to him. He desires for you to live free of fear (John 8:36).

Whether or not you use makeup is for you and your parents to decide. However, don't equate going without any makeup to being spiritual. Wearing no makeup *can* be a sign of simply being unkempt (unless your skin, nails, hair and clothing are neatly tended to).

> Slipshod grooming only attracts slipshod guys
> (and does not glorify the Lord).

Now, with all the variety in guys, some prefer the no-makeup look! At least part of the time. One guy enthusiastically said, "I love camp because that's when you find out who the quality girls are!" He meant that girls are more likely to appear natural—and be themselves—in a roughing-it setting where it's almost impossible to be impeccably groomed. That's when girls with a sense of humor and a sparkling personality really shine. And guys love joyful girls!

Sense of Humor

Sometimes messiness can be more an attitude than an appearance. A girl can be muddy, have messed-up hair, and need a shower, but if it's because she's been tubing down the river at camp, having a great time and being friendly, the guys may gently tease, but what they are really noticing is something entirely different than her appearance. That's one of those times when guys think a *lot* but don't say it. Though she isn't all dolled up at that moment, the guys are taking note of her inner beauty—her glowing personality. She may look really messy outwardly, but they find her personality refreshing. As much as guys like well-groomed girls, they know that camp is one of many occasions when perfect grooming isn't always possible. In those instances, guys could care less about a little temporary messiness when they're around a girl who's fun to be with.

> Guys like it when girls enjoy life and don't take themselves too seriously.

To them, a girl's easy laughter and joyful freedom is absolutely beautiful. (Not to be confused with flirtatious teasing.) Guys are easily able to distinguish the difference between a girl who is just plain sloppy and one who looks disheveled because she's having fun in an outdoor setting. Some guys are going to find your pink-from-the-cold nose or that strand of hair stuck to your sweaty, dirt-smeared-but-smiling face truly adorable!

That brings two young ladies to mind. They are both absolutely charming. There are usually guys around them, so I guess that's not just my opinion. Both girls are well-groomed. But they also are outgoing and able to have fun without worrying about how they look, whether they're swinging from a tree rope into a river, riding horses or engaging in a youth group prank. I hear the guys' comments. They not only like and enjoy these girls; they respect them.

It doesn't matter if it's nature settings, highly formal occasions or somewhere in between, guys appreciate girls who radiate joy and have a healthy sense of humor. (There's a difference between that and being silly, by the way.)

> Girls with sullen or haughty expressions are a turnoff to guys, no matter how pretty a girl is.

Vicki worked in an office with Mona, a young lady who was model-beautiful. Mona wore fashionable clothes. Her makeup was perfect; the way she moved was perfect. Everything about her seemed perfect. Vicki felt jealous but was also intrigued by Mona and wanted to be her friend. But Vicki was reluctant to approach her because Mona rarely smiled, and she didn't initiate conversations with Vicki. Then Vicki began noticing that Mona didn't socialize much with other coworkers either. She was usually alone.

One day Vicki overheard a conversation between Mona and another girl in the office. She learned that Mona was unhappy about not having dates. It made sense to Vicki. If she felt hindered from knowing Mona because of her chilling demeanor, guys probably did too.

Guys may stare at model-perfect girls but they're not attracted to aloof haughtiness. They're reluctant to approach those girls. That's one reason some beautiful girls find themselves alone.

> Part of the reason guys like cheerful girls is because men carry the weight of ultimate leadership on their shoulders.

Because of this, guys find encouragement in being around girls who are relaxed and pleasant. It helps lighten their load and is a wonderful haven from the stresses of life. Think of it this way: after the football game is over, the guys like to get together with the cheerleaders. Right? They're done with the grueling guy stuff and are eager to forget it for a while. Your smile and positive attitude can mean a lot to a guy who needs encouraging. You might even want to try it on your dad. See if it doesn't cheer him up when you give him an upbeat greeting.

Humility

Guys are attracted to humble girls like bees to honey. The two fun-loving girls mentioned above are examples of girls with humility. They like themselves enough to care about the way they look but aren't so caught up with their appearance that it hinders them from enjoying activities with others. Mona the office worker, on the other hand, is an example of the drawbacks that come with pride. She was way too focused on perfecting the outward, and her attempts to attract guys were the very things that turned them away.

Of course, not all quiet people are snotty. But an observer is often left guessing whether a silent person is very shy or simply self-absorbed. One tip-off is the combination of a flawless appearance coupled with a cold attitude toward others. Even if it's not intentional, a girl like that is communicating pride, an I'm-better-than-you, it's-all-about-me message. That's the way guys read it anyway.

If you struggle with shyness, constantly focus on your appearance or are afraid to let people see you with a hair out of place, there are ways to overcome this. Everyone wants to be accepted, not just you. If you focus on putting others at ease, it becomes easier to forget about yourself. Concentrating on making a difference in other people's lives is an invigorating way to become free of self-consciousness.

> The more you reach out to help others feel comfortable, the more you'll be liked, and the less you'll feel the need to perfect yourself to be accepted.

With that approach, everybody wins.

Sometimes, though, it isn't shyness; it's plain old pride. Self-absorbed girls are disgusting to guys. (Aren't *you* turned off when *they're* egotistical?) Pride shows in a number of ways. Here's a little (and only partial) checklist:

- Unwillingness to associate or be seen with people who aren't in your class or group of friends
- Thinking you're doing a guy a favor by talking to him
- Judging people by the brand names and styles of their clothing
- Feeling superior to others based on *your* opinion of your beauty (or your intelligence)
- Reveling in attention from lots of guys, constantly flirting . . .

You get the picture. Quality guys are eager to keep their distance from girls like this.

When it comes to explaining the humility that guys are so attracted to in girls, it's sometimes easier to describe what humility *isn't*. Cattiness is an example. It's an action that guys especially despise in females—girls gossiping behind other girls' backs, putting each other down. Guys find it particularly repulsive. And immature. To guys, that habit makes even the prettiest girls look ugly.

Brad was part of a group of girls and guys that often spent time together. Once when he had occasion to be with them the better part of a whole day, he saw a side to the girls (all of whom were exceptionally attractive) that he'd never seen before. For *hours* he heard the girls gossip. They picked apart a whole host of other girls and guys he knew. That was the last time Brad associated with those girls. He was so disgusted that he distanced himself from them permanently. He never said anything to the girls about how he felt. They still probably don't know why he stopped hanging with them.

Guys do like to be around joy-filled girls, but it's a complete turnoff when the girls are laughing about other people. As much as I've heard guys talk about this, only guys know how *often* they lose respect for girls who are snotty. This is a point that definitely shouldn't remain a secret.

Since cattiness is particularly ugly to guys, you can see why they are so drawn to girls who speak kindly. I overheard a bunch of guys talking among themselves about a girl like this:

"Autumn is nice to everyone."

"I've never heard her say anything mean about anyone."

"Yeah, I really like her."

That young lady has no idea what an impression she made on those guys. But in their spare time, she was the center of their attention! In both these instances . . .

[It was not outward beauty that determined
the girls' level of appeal to the guys.]

If this is an area in your life that you feel you need to work on, the book of Proverbs in the Bible is loaded with verses about the power of the tongue. You can find help and hope by studying and memorizing those Scriptures.

Along with noticing gossip, guys also quickly figure out which girls jockey for position among themselves. Competing to be the most popular might bring a little temporary satisfaction, but at what cost? When girls step on each other in order to rise to the top, guys catch on. And they're not favorably impressed.

Humility rejoices when others are blessed. Being at peace with yourself when other girls are in the limelight is a sure sign that you're walking in humility. Even though you might feel invisible during those times, you might be surprised if you knew who is noticing your peaceful (and beautiful) countenance!

Holiness

Along with humility, guys are awed by holiness in a girl. Not a holier-than-thou attitude, but the beauty that radiates from a girl who spends time with the Lord and lives to please him. That kind of beauty is anything but standoffish. A girl who lives close to the Lord emanates the fruit of the Spirit (Galatians 5:22, 23) and everyone can see it, not just the guys. It's visible!

We see examples of this in both the Old and New Testaments. When Moses came down from Mount Sinai after spending time with the Lord, all the people saw that his face was radiant (Exodus 34:29-35). This also happened for Stephen: "All who were sitting in the Sanhedrin looked intently at Stephen, and they saw that his face was like the face of an angel" (Acts 6:15). According to the Bible, there is a beauty about holiness (see 1 Chronicles 16:29, KJV; Psalm 29:2, KJV; Psalm 96:9, KJV). Wouldn't it be wonderful to have *that* said about you!

[
Living in harmony with the Lord actually
enhances your physical appearance!
]

If you're thinking the examples of Moses and Stephen are isolated cases limited to Bible characters, I should tell you that I've seen varying degrees of this "beauty of holiness" many times. (If you stop and think about it, you'll probably realize that you have too.)

As a new Christian, I was thrilled when I led a neighbor girl to the Lord. The timing of her conversion coincided with a conference on the Holy Spirit that was coming to our community, and she enthusiastically accepted when I invited her to attend with me. On the way home from those meetings one night, her joy was unmistakable. She was absolutely bubbly, expressing delight in her newfound Savior. It was dark in the car but I was amazed to see that her face was shining—it glowed!

Since then, I have seen that same radiance many times in people who love the Lord. It's not always a literal glow but sometimes simply a beauty that transcends the physical. Perhaps this is easier for you to identify if you think of people whom you know or have heard of— their before-meeting-the-Lord and after-meeting-the-Lord appearance. Huge difference, isn't there?

I've also seen what happens to the outward appearance of people who fall away from the Lord. Their special "beauty of holiness" disappears. The Bible even describes this: "When thou with rebukes dost correct man for iniquity, thou makest his beauty to consume away like a moth" (Psalm 39:11, KJV). They revert back to a flat and unattractive appearance when they depart from the Lord—even people noted for their outstanding looks—their "light" is gone.

But the opposite is true as well. You've heard of beauty makeovers, right? Ceci is a lady who was discontent with her appearance. She was bored with her hairstyle and wanted a new overall look. So even though she felt a little silly, she decided to pray about it. She asked the Lord if he would be willing to give her a beauty makeover. To her amazement and delight, he did just that.

The first change came when she began to feel a new yearning to draw closer to the Lord. She responded by spending more time with him. As she grew more serious about being obedient to God, other changes took place. One day she picked up a pair of scissors and began snipping away at her hair. (I'm NOT suggesting you do that!) Then she started experimenting with her curling iron. Before long, she had a new hairstyle that she loved! It was a style she *never* would have considered—she was too certain it wouldn't work with her type of hair. But it did! And she received overwhelming compliments. When Ceci realized that God cared about such ordinary details in her life, she loved him all the more. She was experiencing some of the practical side benefits of the "beauty of holiness."

Even though holiness is an inner condition that also shows on the outside, it's the heart motive, that inner glow, that draws guys! They like being around girls who emanate peace and serenity. It's soothing to a guy, very attractive.

Individuality

Guys are fascinated by unique girls. Some females just seem to have a certain charisma about them that guys are quick to notice. That winsomeness often comes from daring to be different, from not being a cookie-cutter version of everyone else, from not always following the crowd.

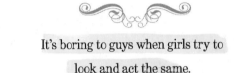

> It's boring to guys when girls try to look and act the same.

Often girls' attempts at a certain look are patterned after the latest female pop star. But let's face it, that pop star is unique. She has her own look. It's her distinctiveness that makes her notable—or notorious. When you try to copy her, you're placing yourself in the precarious position of being *compared* to *her*, instead of having your own identity. That doesn't work very well for several reasons.

In the first place, you're not going to measure up to her because you aren't her. It's impossible to be someone else. Second, why would you *want* to look like her? Too often those role models are far from godly examples, far from what God has in mind for you. Third, the quality guys have already seen her and (don't forget) are *not* impressed.

One great-looking guy told me that even when guys think a certain pop star is hot to look at, they don't listen to her music. They don't take her seriously. To guys she's simply a bit of eye candy—a little temporary treat—but nothing to consider for a lifetime commitment. Her fans are mostly female.

> When we understand the way guys think, we
> realize that even if a girl succeeds in copying a
> celebrity, she only impresses other girls—not the
> guys! Guys are looking for someone unique . . .

someone who stands out from the rest. That is *so* in your favor!

In God's infinite creativity, he designed you to be unique—different from any other girl on this planet! Just think, there is not another you in the entire universe! Isn't it exciting to be elite, a one-of-a-kind girl? That's something to celebrate. It's certainly something guys celebrate. That is, *if* you let your individuality show!

Why not ask God to reveal who he created *you* to be. When you begin to embrace the look and personality that God had in mind especially for you, you'll be far more appealing than when trying to model yourself after someone else. Isn't it thrilling to know you have your own customized look? Capitalize on it!

Unique Beauty

Discover what your special features are. Whether it's curly or straight hair, the color of your eyes, the color of your skin, high cheek bones, dimples, freckles . . . even unusual features which you might wish were different can actually become one of your beauty points. Many celebrities are famous for their exceptional appearance, which is often from a more notable feature—a nose, a generous smile, blazing red hair, prominent chin, long neck, baby-doll lips . . . People find the unusual stunning. The very feature you may dread can become a lovely focal point.

> Decide what characteristics make you unique
> and ask God to help you not only accept them
> but also highlight them!

Often, the only difference in whether or not people find you attractive is in your attitude toward yourself. Sarah was extremely self-conscious about her nose and would have given just about anything to have a smaller one. That is, until she received compliments on her nose from a guy! She was astonished to think that *that* could be what made her attractive! She kept thinking about what he said. Then she began to notice certain celebrities with different noses; it was their noses that gave them their distinctive beauty! Sarah's whole attitude about herself changed, and she began to actually enjoy her unique look. It was fun to be different.

Unique Talents

It's not just your appearance that's one-of-a-kind. God has also given each person certain gifts and interests tailored to form her individual personality. Everyone has them—no exceptions. That means you too! All of us have a measure of creativity. We put it into action in different ways, sometimes without even realizing it. If you're not sure what your talents are, ask the Lord to help you discover them. They could very well have something to do with what you already enjoy doing. And they also will be a blessing to the world. "For we are God's workmanship, created in Christ Jesus to do good works, which God prepared in advance for us to do" (Ephesians 2:10). Isn't that incredible?

[God doesn't make mistakes.]

Any artist knows that what she creates, whether it's drawing, dancing, music or some other form of expression, comes from within her heart. Even someone with a gift of administration and organization must use her imagination in order to structure her plans. Once we understand that those creative gifts come from within us, we can begin to understand what specially created beings we are, brought forth out of God's flawless imagination of pure love (1 John 4:16)!

So what if you don't want to try out for cheerleading! Not all guys want to be on the football team either. Guys enjoy diversity. What is it *you* enjoy doing? Even if it's something more unusual—like tying flies for fishing or raising sheep—there are guys who would love to have an intelligent conversation with a girl who understands and is interested in those things.

Besides being male, guys are people. Like everyone else, they appreciate being with others whom they can feel comfortable around. When asked what his dream girl would be like, one young man said, "A girl that is goal-oriented and knows what she wants to do . . . she doesn't necessarily have to look great, but she has to be attractive—someone I can actually talk to and have conversation with."

At an age when guys are easily impressed by what they see, this fifteen-year-old guy already knew he wanted more than looks. His dream girl would be a kindred spirit, someone with whom he could share his heart in conversation. It will take a special girl with a unique personality to be his soul mate. How perfectly wonderful to be an original!

Have we covered everything guys find beautiful? Of course not!

That's what makes this so fun. I've highlighted a few things here, but guys' secrets about the intriguing subject of beauty are tucked throughout this whole book! In fact, some things about girls are so captivating to guys, they deserve their own chapter. Like this next one . . .

Secret No. 3

Guys Love a Little Mystery

Lana has a knack for rocking a guy's world. Other girls who see her in the mall probably pass her by, never guessing she can make a guy's head spin. Yes, she's nice looking, but not totally gorgeous. She's well-groomed but her hairstyle is not terribly in. Her clothing is beautiful but not the trendiest, and it's certainly not revealing. Besides that, Lana is rather quiet and definitely doesn't flirt. In other words, to look at her in a room full of people, nothing would come to mind that makes her stand out from anyone else. Yet, when she enters a room, there's an immediate commotion among the guys! When they spot her, the guys start looking at each other and grinning. Even some of the married men straighten their ties and stand a little taller. Why is that? Whether she knows it or not, Lana has captured the essence of a secret that guys really love. She's an expert at maintaining a mystery about her.

Years ago, the founder of a Bible college gave some advice to a friend of mine. With a twinkle in his eyes, this dignified man of God shared a valuable secret: "Always keep a little mystery about yourself."

My sons agree. I've lost count of the times I've heard them and their friends express great enthusiasm over upcoming social events where there will be new girls to meet. You should see the guys! Youth conferences, interchurch activities, school, community events such as county fairs and holiday celebrations—any opportunities to encounter girls they haven't met before—are looked forward to by the guys with bright anticipation.

Now it isn't as if these events were the only occasions when guys socialize with girls. They're around girls all the time, and many of those girls are close friends with the guys. So what's all the fuss? Well, let me put it to you like this—

> Guys like a little mystery. Actually, they *really* like it! They're fascinated by the unknown; it presents a challenge.

Guys love a challenge. Even something as simple as trying to open a tightly sealed jar can temporarily sidetrack all four of the guys in our home. If some of their friends happen to be around, they quickly jump into the fray. That jar is jostled from guy to guy until someone eventually gets it open, at which time every guy claims to have been the one who loosened the lid.

Guys by nature are conquerors. Just look at their interest in football, video games, rock climbing—all sports, actually—anything that presents an obstacle to overcome. Oftentimes, the tougher the challenge, the better they like it. This includes the challenge that some girls present.

Now, the kind of "conquering" I'm referring to doesn't mean that guys want to belittle or defeat a girl. I am talking about the enjoyable quest a guy embarks upon in trying to master his curiosity about her!

[
Where there's a mystery surrounding a girl,
there'll be a guy who wants to solve it!
]

Most of the time, though, guys wish girls were *more* of a challenge. Our culture has become so casual and informal that, for guys, much of the wonderful mystery about females has been lost. Girls whom the guys already know have become so familiar there's often not enough of the unknown left. It's the secrets that keep guys interested. This is why new situations with different girls are so much more intriguing.

You know what happens when a new girl comes on the scene, don't you? I'm sure you've seen it. At school, church, the neighborhood, wherever—guys are alert to any new young lady. Her very presence initiates a fresh commotion because *she's* a mystery. If the new girl knows how to maintain her mystery, she'll remain a challenge. If not, she eventually becomes another of the girls that the guys know too well. And the guys move on, looking for the next mysterious female.

Please don't be offended. This doesn't mean guys are rejecting their female friends or that their friendship with you isn't genuine. It just means that much of the edge that *could* be there is missing. The guys wish it was still there. Since guys love a little mystery, those new situations with unfamiliar girls are bound to pique their curiosity.

Though this next example is extreme, it's a delightful case of a girl who maintained a mystery about herself.

Sunny

Sunny is a girl who made an unusual decision to exclude guys from her life. She wanted to pursue the Lord and didn't want the distractions that many teenagers face with boy-girl relationships. For various other reasons as well, she simply decided not even to talk to guys. It wasn't her goal to deliberately snub them; she wasn't being snotty. She just kept herself busy with school, youth group and other female friends. When guys came around her group, she quietly walked away. With that scenario, you can imagine how the guys reacted. Here was a real challenge! More than one guy made it his mission to try to get Sunny to at least talk to him!

Behind the scenes, the guys discussed among themselves their success—actually, lack of success—at getting her to speak. There may have been more, but I heard of only one guy whom Sunny talked with. If there were others, they must have been few and far between. She never dated.

She went all the way through high school with her guy-free resolve. Finally, when she had grown into a beautiful young lady, a very special guy came along—a real prince of a guy—someone as special as Sunny, and they became friends. This young man could have chosen from any number of girls who gladly gave him their attention. Yet he set his sights on quiet, elusive Sunny.

Their friendship grew as they talked, and he eventually captured her heart. Her eyes sparkled at their wedding reception, and this young man's adoration for his bride was obvious. Think of the triumph for this guy! He won a pure young lady, poised, mature and devoted to the Lord. To this day, Sunny quietly maintains an aura of mystery about her that continues to radiate beauty. Her husband seems anything but bored!

Sunny's intention was not to create mystery, yet her actions absolutely had that effect on the guys. Other girls can have that magnetism too, without having to do anything as drastic.

> The secret is for girls to know how to be friends with guys while still maintaining some mystery.

That way, they present the kind of challenge that guys love to take on. What can guys conquer or pursue if girls reveal everything about themselves? I'm referring to how you relate to guys, but it also applies to how you dress.

Mystery in Dress

Uh-oh. Here comes that word again. It might seem like I'm harping on the issue of modesty but how can I keep this delightful info to myself? If girls understood the mystique and attraction created by dressing demurely, they'd gladly overhaul their wardrobes. They wouldn't even dream of voluntarily relinquishing their power by showing "everything they've got."

> Mystery is created by concealing, not by revealing!

We all love receiving gifts, don't we? Doesn't it make the gift more exciting if it's wrapped? The wrapping adds to the mystery and increases our anticipation, especially if we have to wait some time before being able to open the gift. Doesn't it raise the suspense even more when the gift is beautifully wrapped? Often, the wrapping is an indicator of the value of the gift inside.

When you receive an exquisitely wrapped gift—think Christmas here for a minute—doesn't it drive you nuts with curiosity? Wouldn't a large part of the fun be lost if your parents (and everyone else) piled everything under the tree unwrapped? Day after day until December 25, those gifts would be on display for everybody to see. Anyone could view the presents meant for them and also the gifts intended for everyone else. There'd be no secrets, no surprises and no suspense.

To males, females are much like gifts. Each male knows that someday one of those females may be his wife. Alongside wanting to avoid temptation, that's another powerful reason why guys wish girls would dress modestly. Every guy wants to know that his girl is exclusively his. He wants to enjoy her secrets but isn't willing to share them with other guys. Every guy prefers that his "gift" be wrapped. It's the unknown, the what-is-hidden, that is enticing.

If a girl displays her body for all the guys to look at, she has removed the "wrapping." She is showing and giving away her treasure that is supposed to be saved for just one man. That doesn't happen only when a girl has sex with a guy; it applies also when her clothing reveals too much of her body. When a girl dresses that way, she has far less to present to her future husband alone.

> [Like unwrapped gifts under a Christmas tree,
> many girls today have no secrets,
> no surprises and no suspense.]

The guys have already seen it all—and wish they hadn't—because in their hearts the guys know that each girl is someone else's intended gift.

That's sad. But, it doesn't have to *stay* that way. Mystery can be restored. If you find you've been giving away your secrets by the way you dress, simply make some changes. It's never too late to once again be cloaked in mystery. And, isn't it exciting to think that some guy might consider *you* a gift?

Let's talk about wrapping for a minute. I don't want to take this analogy too far but . . . a gift covered with plain brown paper, a raffia bow and a sprig of pine can be exquisitely wrapped. It doesn't need to have shiny foil paper and glittery ribbon to be beautiful. The same is true for girls. They don't need expensive brand-name clothing to be exquisitely "wrapped" either. To some guys, the simple-but-elegant, natural look is a knockout!

We can't all throw out our wardrobes and start over, although I do know of a young lady who did almost exactly that. She got rid of a large part of her wardrobe, discarding miniskirts and figure-hugging clothing—even photographs of herself wearing those items—not because anyone told her to do it. But after she made a decision to follow Christ, she found that she *wanted* to dress differently.

Even if we have unlimited funds, finding the right things isn't always easy right away. It takes a little time to retrain your eyes to spot clothing that fits you—spirit, soul and body! And it requires some imagination. But it can be done. It's not really that complicated. Sometimes all it takes is adding a layer—a top over your T, for example.

I want to challenge you to consider adding something else to your wardrobe too. You might think I'm crazy for saying this, but you may be surprised at the reaction you'll get from guys simply by wearing a dress or skirt sometimes. Oh, I know there are already occasions where you wear them, but you have to admit, it's not very often anymore, right? Not for everyday attire anyway. And that's exactly what I'm suggesting. I mean everyday occasions like going to the store, school, youth group—being out in public, in general. I'd like to challenge you to try wearing a casual dress or skirt outfit for any occasion where you might normally wear jeans.

Nope. Miniskirts, skimpy, tight-fitting tops, see-through fabrics and little-nothing dresses don't count. Neither does ultratailored business attire. Find a casual dress or skirt and top. Nothing real dressy, but something you like and can feel comfortable wearing. (OK, if you hardly *ever* wear a dress, maybe nothing is going to make you feel very comfortable, but give it a try anyway.) Since this is a challenge, maybe you'll want to start out by stopping in at a consignment or thrift shop. That way it won't cost much to give this little endeavor a whirl.

Wash and iron your garments to freshen them. Then show up wearing your outfit where you'd normally wear jeans. When they see you, guys are likely to ask why you're dressed that way. By all means, don't tell them you're conducting an experiment and they're the guinea pigs! Keep the mystery. Just give 'em a vague answer like, "Because I want to." And smile.

You're missing out on some special girl fun if you don't wear skirts for non-occasions every so often. Donning skirts and dresses is still exclusive to females and we need to enjoy it. I didn't say exploit it; we're not talking seductive here. I'm talking about relishing your femininity.

See if you don't enjoy the difference in the way you're treated when you start wearing skirts and dresses instead of pants in casual settings once in a while.

[
A young lady wearing a dress has a way of bringing out the best in guys.
]

It inspires men to respect themselves more and challenges them to exhibit better manners. They'll treat you like a lady and with more respect. You'll likely feel better about yourself as well.

Not *that* long ago, women wore dresses all the time. It has only been since the end of World War II that women started wearing pants on a regular basis. Actually, it was really later than that—more like the 1960s and '70s.

Making dresses and skirts a normal part of your wardrobe is another way to exert your individuality and your originality because not many girls are doing this—yet! I expect skirts and dresses are going to make a comeback—big time! Here's an opportunity for you to *lead* a trend instead of following! And wearing dresses is another very powerful and effective way to restore some of your mystery.

Mystery in Conduct

It is possible to be too open and too buddy-buddy with guys. There seems to be a fine line between treating them as brothers in the Lord and crossing over into *too* familiar territory.

[
When a guy knows everything about you,
it leaves nothing for him to conquer.
]

Here are a few questions you can ask yourself to see if you're keeping some mystery:

Who initiates most of the conversations I have with a guy?

If it's you, you might want to back off a bit. How can you be sure which guys are interested unless you give them the opportunity to approach you first? Here's an example:

Myles had been out of town attending school. When he came home for a visit, everyone at church was thrilled to see him. Especially the girls! One beaming girl after another bounced over to Myles, greeting him with hugs and enthusiastic chatter. He accepted their hugs, smiling and listening to each of them. But he never moved from where he stood. He didn't have to. The girls made a steady stream over to him.

Now, don't misunderstand. It's great to welcome home a friend. But on that evening the girls stood out as the aggressors. As popular as Myles was with the guys too, they were strangely absent from that welcoming scene. Were his male friends glad to see him? Absolutely! But they had a much more laid-back approach to getting reacquainted with him. And they were very likely trying to stay out of the girls' way.

Let's rewind this scene and brainstorm for a minute. How could the girls have expressed a friendly welcome home to Myles with more discretion?

• How about a friendly wave from across the room? That gives *him* the opportunity to walk over to a girl if he wants to talk with her.

• Instead of one-on-one greetings, the girls could blend in a bit more by approaching in small groups. Hmmm. Maybe. But a group of girls cornering him could feel intimidating.

• A girl could suggest to a mutual guy friend that he go with her to greet Myles.

• Is there an event planned to welcome him home? Waiting for that may require some restraint, but poised young women can do that. Especially when they're working on maintaining mystery!

• How about expressing your pleasure in seeing him again, but without the hugs? We'll talk more about this later, but all those female hugs were more stimulation than Myles needed to deal with. In addition to the physical aspects, giving away hugs too freely decreases their value.

> Hugging guys is often where girls cross that
> invisible line into too familiar territory. Females
> with mystery don't do that.

Make yourself and your hugs precious by saving them for a special guy.

Who initiates our activities, the girls or the guys?
Depending on the rules in her home about dating or courting, a girl

can feel at times that her social life looks bleak. Especially if she thinks adults aren't planning enough girl-guy activities. That's when girls are tempted to take matters into their own hands. And they often do.

Hey, it's natural for females to plan social events! As adults, it usually is the women who make most of the arrangements. But as single young people, when girls are predominantly the initiators for social gatherings, the guys have varying responses. Occasionally, they're delighted. But when invitations become too numerous and the girls always seem to be in charge, guys become weary of the pace. In those cases, they'll either attend out of obligation or opt not to show up. That's a far cry from the enthusiasm they show when having an opportunity to meet "mysterious" girls.

Keep the mystery. Let the guys go awhile without your initiating something. Believe me, they will definitely figure out a way to mingle with girls again!

Who's making the phone calls?

Explosive question, isn't it? Let's tackle it anyway. If you're expecting to hear that you should never call a guy, you can relax. There are too many variables on this issue to say never. But here are a couple things to think about before you pick up the phone.

If you make the first call, you can't be confident of his degree of interest in you.

Isn't it more difficult to develop a genuine relationship with a guy when you're not really sure where you stand with him? Most guys won't be rude if you call, so it's easy to mistake a guy's polite phone manners for personal interest in you. That's what happened to Michelle.

She had a huge crush on Ross. At school, she left notes in his school books telling him to phone her. When he didn't, she started calling him. Wanting to be polite, Ross took time to chat with her. I'm sure you can guess what happened. Michelle misinterpreted Ross's courtesy as interest and began calling him more often. Sometimes several times a day. Her boldness grew into a nightmare for Ross and ultimately his family. When the phone rang, he'd cringe and race outdoors, asking family members to say he wasn't in. After all, he didn't want to lie.

In a television sitcom, this story might make us laugh. But for Ross, it wasn't funny. Michelle's persistent calls stopped only after Ross's parents stepped in. How embarrassing for everyone!

That was all so unnecessary. Michelle is an attractive girl. All she needs is to learn a few secrets about guys—one of them being to keep some mystery in her conduct.

Without realizing it, your phone call could end a potential friendship with a young man before it begins.

Guys want to be conquerors, remember? *But what if he seems too shy to make the first move? Shouldn't you help him out a little in a case like that?*

Dustin was athletic, a great student, and he enjoyed girl watching. But he wasn't a "player." Plenty of girls had communicated their availability to him, but he wasn't interested. Their eager signals posed no challenge. He was content instead to enjoy his freedom and concentrate on his future. Until the day he spotted Sage. After that, the future he concentrated on was spelled S-a-g-e!

Sage was calm, peaceful and soft spoken. Her poised presence emanated a quiet maturity that Dustin admired. To him, she was totally beautiful; he desperately wanted to meet her. But with his new interest came a big problem, one that Dustin hadn't confronted before. He was scared! At last, this conqueror was confronted with something—some-one—that made him quake.

I better tell you here that Sage noticed Dustin too. From a distance, she caught him looking at her and she smiled. But she made no effort to introduce herself. She continued going about life with her friends. Sage was often in the same places as Dustin; if he wanted to approach her, he could. But he never did. How frustrating.

Meanwhile, Dustin lived life in a daze. He desperately wanted to meet this lovely girl, but how to get up the nerve? What should he say? What if she thought he was a dork? How do you introduce yourself to someone out of the clear blue? Don't you need a reason to speak to a girl? How do you break the ice? Dustin agonized for days, then weeks. He mentally rehearsed conversations, but each time the opportunity came to actually speak to Sage, he froze. Days turned into months!

> Few girls understand the depths of turmoil a guy experiences when he's interested in a girl.

If a girl catches on and she's interested in that guy, it can become agony for her too. That's when she has to decide whether or not to try help-ing out the guy. In Sage's case, she did exactly the right thing. Nothing. Well, except maybe occasionally to be in the right place at the right time.

Finally the day came when Dustin determined to speak to Sage—no matter what! And he did. Just like that. He introduced himself and their conversation began. For Dustin, it was a rite of passage and a mighty sweet victory.

Wouldn't it have been a whole lot easier on everyone if Sage had just said something first? Was it really all that necessary for them both to go through so much emotional turmoil? Actually, yes, it was! For a couple reasons.

Plenty of girls had been friendly toward Dustin. Problem was, they were *too* familiar. If Sage had decided to try to help him out by making the first move, it would have brought an end to his interest in her. His life was already loaded with available girls; he was looking for a rare catch.

Also, when it comes to guys conquering, sometimes what they most need to conquer is themselves!

If you step in at the wrong time, intending to help a guy out, you may be interfering with his inner battle, taking away his opportunity for victory.

You know what that does? It forces him either to surrender leadership to you or to look elsewhere until he *can* master his fear! Dustin's pursuit of Sage wasn't all about her. It was partly about him!

Dustin wasn't by nature a shy guy. But when it came to being around a girl that rocked his world, he *became* shy! A guy's uncharacteristic shyness around you *may* be a sign of his interest. If you think there's a shy guy interested but he seems afraid to approach you, instead of helping him out, why not pray for him? Ask God to give him the courage he needs to be a conqueror.

Does he ask questions, or do I volunteer information?

Asking yourself this question periodically can help you become more aware of the circumstances surrounding your relationships with guys. It's like a gauge or thermometer for measuring his interest factor. And your mystery level!

There's no doubt that guys respond to girls who pursue them. Some guys even say they like it. Their reason?

"Because it takes the pressure off."

"I feel more comfortable."

Some guys today are willing for girls to pursue them because of the overload of pressure guys already feel from female competition and put-downs. (We'll look at this more in Secret No. 5, "Guys vs. Girls.") They feel it just makes life easier to let the girls lead the chase.

Maybe you can think of a relationship which is working out fine even though a girl initiated it. I can too. That's why I said there are too many variables to say never. But when it comes to pursuing a guy, let's look at one more question.

Have I looked at what this means in my future?

Suppose you do make the first move, and things develop into a close relationship. Imagine the guy is delighted; he's enjoying your pursuit. You're having fun together and you like that he's so willing to go along with your plans. By being the aggressor and making the first move, you may be setting a precedent for your relationship.

OK, now keep imagining . . . into your future . . . marriage . . . children. You have chosen a guy who is allowing you to be the leader. That means you're in charge. When children come along, and your leadership role becomes too burdensome, would it be fair to expect your husband to suddenly become the leader? Would that be a reasonable expectation? At that point, would it be logical to become angry with him for letting you carry the bulk of responsibility? Or did the real problem begin years before?

Even guys with leadership qualities will often respond to girls who pursue them. They may spend time with those girls and do things with them. But when it comes right down to it, and guys find a girl that they are genuinely interested in, they *will* pursue her. In the meantime, they lightheartedly enjoy the fact that other girls want to be with them. But it doesn't necessarily mean they're interested on a romantic level. They're just kind of filling their time. Girls who don't understand the status of these relationships can end up feeling hurt.

If you're fuming mad right now, please don't be. I'm telling you these secrets so you can avoid this kind of hurt. Wouldn't you rather know the obstacles you may encounter when girls chase the guys?

Besides, there *is* a flip side to this issue. If you have a clear picture of the nature of your relationship with a guy, a casual friendship can be wonderful. So don't abandon your guy friends. And don't think they're being jerks. It's great to have "brothers" who can help you navigate the world of guys (as long as you remember that they are, after all, guys)! That's often the environment where trust and genuine bonding occur—and where romance can bud—provided you keep some mystery!

Secret No. 4

Guys Are Not All Alike

It was more than a courtesy thing. It was what best buds do—bail each other out. That's why Lance agreed to endure Ben's family reunion with him for the weekend.

Now it's a little complicated, but this is the reason Ben wanted Lance to go: Ben's cousin had come to town for the reunion. He'd grown up with her. They'd been like brother and sister until he moved. Of course, Ben was looking forward to seeing her again, but there'd been a lot changes in four years. Ben had a girlfriend now and she'd be with him at the family gathering. Spending time with his cousin just wouldn't be the same as before.

So Lance, being the good bro that he was, said he'd join them to make it a foursome—but with a firm stipulation. Ben had to promise not to ditch Lance, leaving him alone with his sister-type cousin. Fortified with Ben's assurance, Lance tagged along to the opening event, the

Friday night reception.

"There she is." Ben nodded toward the doorway and then started walking across the reception hall toward his cousin. "Hmmm. She's grown up! Maybe I'm doing *you* the favor, Lance," Ben cracked, tossing the words over his shoulder as he walked hand-in-hand with his girlfriend.

"Lance?" Ben turned, expecting a witty reply from his buddy. Lance was still standing by the punch table, the spot from where Ben had first pointed out his cousin. But Lance's gaze was already past Ben and his girlfriend, fixed on the young lady standing just inside the doorway.

Her light brown hair was short and curly—girls might see it as somewhat old-ladyish—but Lance noticed her regal posture and slender neck.

The older man standing beside her spoke and she nodded. Then she obviously caught sight of Ben because she waved gracefully in their direction. Turning to the gentleman that Lance guessed must be her dad, she gave him a hug and a kiss on the cheek and then started walking toward Ben.

She was wearing a long-sleeved top made out of some kind of shiny fabric; the color of the ocean on an overcast day, Lance thought. As she got closer, he noticed pearl buttons down its front and at the cuffs. Her gently swinging black skirt stopped about five inches above her shoes—black, strapped sandals with teeny heels—revealing little more than her delicate ankles.

"Dude," Ben elbowed Lance, "what's your problem?"

Startled, Lance stared back at his buddy, wishing like crazy he could stop the blush he felt creeping up his face.

Ben grinned. "C'mon, man. I want you to meet my cousin Lana."

The threesome headed toward her as Lance whispered, "Hey, Ben, about that promise . . . don't feel obligated . . ."

OK, push the pause button here. We'd already met Lana, in the last chapter, remember? But we hadn't met Lance yet. She just rocked his world, but all we know so far about this guy is that he's best friends with Ben. What is he really like?

That's a good question for girls to ask about any guy they're considering because it's important to understand that not all guys are alike. All it takes is a glance around the school cafeteria or a stroll through the mall to see that. Still, just as advertising, TV and movies have fabricated the perfect girl (that you feel pressure to emulate), they have also created the perfect guy.

If we females are honest, we probably have to admit it's easy to forget that that model guy represents an image; he's an icon to sell products. It's easy to use him as our standard for measuring and comparing other guys, yet he's hardly representative of most guys.

> There's way more to guys than can be summed up
> by stuffing them neatly into one category and then
> expecting them to live up to that image.

It's tough when guys feel compelled to conform to that image, and it's even tougher when guys think that girls expect them to be just like that perfect guy. We've already learned that guys don't buy into the media's image for girls. Guys want the same break from girls. They want the freedom to be real too.

Guys don't like being compared to other guys. They're not all alike, and they're very uncomfortable with the idea of their masculinity being determined by their physique. It can be especially difficult for guys who aren't into sports and athletic pursuits.

Lance is one of those guys. He's a musician. Sensitive or creative might better describe him. Lance has had girlfriends, but since he's a more feelings-oriented guy, they seemed too aggressive; so he decided to be solo, at least until he met Lana. Let's take a closer look at this kind of guy.

Before we check out the different sides of guys, let me remind you that this isn't a scientific breakdown of the male species. These are my observations as a sister, mom and hostess to guys. This won't be a complete list, but it'll get you thinking.

Even here we need to be careful not to box guys in to these categories. Let's get past the stereotypes and look at guys' varying facets without labeling them. These traits differ in degree from guy to guy and most males possess a combination of them instead of just one.

Creative

Creative guys are often very sensitive. They're talented in the arts—music, literature, theatre, design—and are a tremendous gift to the world.

Some people misunderstand ultra-sensitive guys because they try to fit all males into a prefabricated macho mold. When feelings-oriented guys don't fit those expectations, they can be labeled as "gay," given uncomplimentary nicknames and receive teasing or rejection.

> Judgmental people might be more careful with
> their prejudices if they understood that God
> designed some guys to be artistically gifted.

Exodus 35:30-35 tells of the Lord filling certain men with the Spirit of God, endowing them with "skill, ability and knowledge in all kinds of crafts—to make artistic designs for work in gold, silver and bronze, to cut and set stones, to work in wood and to engage in all kinds of artistic craftsmanship . . . as designers, embroiderers in . . . yarn and fine linen, and weavers—all of them master craftsmen and designers." Those abilities are imparted by God for a God-ordained purpose.

Those talents by no means make guys less male. But creative guys *are* often more temperamental because their imaginations are more active. In relationships, these guys can easily feel overwhelmed by assertive girls, of which there are many in our culture today because of its strong emphasis on girls competing with guys. If guys feel trapped in an environment of overbearing or badgering females, they perceive themselves as inadequate and some fall prey to homosexuality. (As the influences of the militant feminist movement have increased, there has been a corresponding increase in homosexuality.)

However, when they find the right girl, ultra-sensitive guys soar in their abilities and accomplishments! They do wonderful things for God. These guys need respect, admiration, affirmation and encouragement. They have an important place in the world as males.

It's fascinating to see what kind of girls artistic young men are attracted to and select for wives. They pick virtuous girls with strong character but who are feminine and have a quiet countenance. These girls are kind, gentle and humble, but also accomplished without being overbearing. Because sensitive guys must be disciplined in order to hone a creative skill, they admire girls who also have exercised the self-control needed to excel in something.

Girls who marry sensitive guys have added benefits. These guys can be wonderfully romantic! They enjoy wooing their ladies with flowers and creative expressions of their love. It's not unusual for them to make time-consuming, elaborate plans to bless their special girls with surprises.

OK, here is where we hit the pause button again. This time we're releasing it and fast forwarding to one month after Ben's family reunion. We're zooming in on a home . . . the doorbell rings . . .

Lana set down her hot cocoa and rose from the cushy recliner where she'd been studying for a chemistry test. Through a side window she caught a glimpse of the tan Willis Florist van and recognized Ray Willis as she opened the door.

"Hi, Lana. Glad I caught you home; this is for you," he said, handing her a florist box.

"For me?"

"Yep," Mr. Willis winked. "Who's the lucky guy?" Without waiting for a reply he added, "Gotta run, see ya."

Lana didn't attempt to answer his question. She just smiled and called after him, "Thank you, Ray."

The door clicked shut behind her as she set the long box on the coffee table, slid off the lavender ribbon and lifted the lid. Sitting on top of the waxy, green florist paper was a small envelope. She picked it up and moved aside the crinkly edges of the paper to discover a bouquet of baby's breath, some fern and one exquisite long-stemmed yellow rose. Then she opened the envelope and slipped out the card.

"It's been one month since we met. I'm celebrating. Lance."

That was the beginning of their romantic courtship. The surprises increased from there, eventually leading to an intricately planned marriage proposal.

Was it difficult at times for Lana to refrain from following the crowd in the way she dressed and the things she did? Yes. Was it frustrating to resist the impulse to flirt and pursue relationships with guys, and instead concentrate on personal goals? Of course it was, sometimes. But was it worth it? What do *you* think?

Like Lana, the right girl can bring out the best in a creative guy.

Studious

These guys aren't real outgoing, socially. They don't notice what is or what isn't in, or else they don't seem to care. They can be happily occupied pursuing a hobby. Some of them work at menial jobs—things like fast-food restaurant workers, cart tenders and grocery baggers.

Though they are easily overlooked by their peers in high school, these young men are often the movers and shakers of the future. They're the guys who make notable and admirable contributions to society because they are goal-setters and are willing to pay the price necessary to achieve those goals. It takes determination, focus, self-discipline, humility and sometimes sacrifice to achieve a goal—all signs of strong character. In many ways, studious guys are mature for their age. Their values are beyond those of many young people their age. Girls miss out on knowing some terrific guys when they appraise these guys by comparing them to society's virtual perfect male. Don't be too hasty in writing off the "invisible" guys.

Before bypassing a bookworm, you might want to discreetly take a second look. Granted, some of these guys are more of a challenge to get to know. A lot of them have their thoughts in books. But almost all of them would love to have someone to talk to about the stuff that goes through their heads. Sometimes these guys have specific subjects in which they are particularly interested. They'd enjoy being able to discuss these topics with a knowledgeable girl.

Wouldn't it be a wonderful relief to have a guy friend who has meaningful values, someone around whom you can be real instead of feeling like you have to impress him? If you take time to know some of these guys, you just might discover a prince-to-be!

"Player"

Casanova, heartbreaker, chick magnet—you know the type—there's always a bevy of girls around him. Can I give you a little insight about guys like this?

> When a guy has a string of girlfriends,
> it doesn't mean that he's having a great time.

Guys who go from girlfriend to girlfriend are usually very restless for entirely different reasons than trying to hunt down the perfect girl. Just as girls can't find their ultimate fulfillment in a guy, guys can't find their total contentment in girls either. That place is reserved for God himself. He is the only one who will never, ever fail us.

Players may appear to be romancing their way through life, but they are searching for something which no girl can supply. That's why, even when a young lady gives a guy everything, it still isn't enough to keep him.

Since you can't know the background of guys you're just meeting, you need to be careful.

> When guys are hurting, some of them use girls as a distraction to forget about painful issues.

The very fact that a guy goes through a lot of girls is a warning sign that he has something else going on in his life, some other agenda. His attention may feel flattering, especially if he's popular, but the real issue for him isn't about solid relationships. And it isn't about you. Don't be deceived into believing you're "the one." Each of his girlfriends undoubtedly thought that too.

Steer clear of these guys. Right now they lack the skills to relate to girls in a healthy way. A player needs time to mature. He needs to develop proper methods for dealing with pain before he is ready to have a special girl in his life. (This can take years, so don't stunt your growth by waiting around for him.)

If I'm not romantically involved, is it OK to just be friends with a guy like this? After all, doesn't he need someone to lead him to Jesus?

All guys need to meet Jesus! But girls trying to evangelize guys is a risky business. Hormones, physical attraction, touch, body language and dozens of other underlying signals can get in the way of a clear presentation of the gospel when it's presented one-on-one between a single girl and a single guy.

Your intentions may be entirely pure, but that's no guarantee the guy will see them—or you—that way. In the life of a player, since girls are already a complication, your attempts to evangelize him can't achieve your good intentions.

When you have a burden for any young man's salvation, your safest role is as an intercessor. Only. He doesn't need to know you're praying. In fact, it's best if he *doesn't* know. That way, the guy will benefit but you'll be protected. And neither of you will face the temptation of being pulled into an unhealthy soul-tie relationship.

God can use your prayers to send the *right* people and situations into this young man's life. Your prayers will help bring salvation, healing and wholeness to him. But . . .

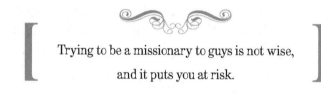

[
Trying to be a missionary to guys is not wise,
and it puts you at risk.
]

Cool Dude

Cool dudes are lovable guys who have succumbed to the pressures of society to present a certain image. Most of them are responsible young men who are trying to live up to the expectations they feel have been placed on them by their peers and their culture. Behind the facades are guys longing to be accepted for who they really are.

I saw a dramatic example of this when some neighbor boys accompanied our family to the lake. I will never forget their change. In town, these three boys were typical cool dudes. They wore cutting-edge, brand-name clothing and did all the stuff popular guys are supposed to do, including displaying a certain level of toughness. They definitely dished out their share of jeering and teasing to other kids. When we invited them along on our family outing, I wasn't sure they'd even want to go and was delighted when they accepted.

Upon arriving at the lake, our sons immediately headed for the water and discovered tadpoles and minnows swimming along the water's grassy edge. In their enthusiasm to catch the creatures, they forgot about being cool around their invited guests, and they splashed along the muddy shore with spirited gusto. That was all the permission the neighbor boys needed to drop their jackets—and their facades—to join the chase.

In that atmosphere, surrounded by nature and uninhibited freedom to enjoy it, those guys had a blast. The tough-guy masks came off, the compulsion to act cool was gone and their real personalities shone through with healthy abandon.

All it took for that transformation was being around people who gave them permission to be themselves. Our boys didn't give that permission intentionally. It was just communicated by example. When our sons were unpretentious, the others also felt free to be themselves.

Once we returned to town, I watched as our three guests morphed back into cool dudes again. It was sad to see they felt compelled to put back on that protective gear. But it was comforting to know that underneath it were three very real guys who I was sure would show up again, given the right environment.

Sometimes people are able to give *themselves* the go-ahead to be real. More commonly though, we live in fear of people's opinions and look to them for that permission.

God has given females a tremendous amount of influence with men. Guys have their own culture and methods of communicating approval or disapproval among themselves. But around females, guys watch girls' responses to them carefully and decide how free they dare to be around those females.

[
One wise way for girls to use their power of influence is by providing an atmosphere of acceptance for guys.
]

Acceptance doesn't mean *approval.* It simply means you withhold judgment. You accept who a guy is, no matter what he is like. You don't have to agree with him or approve of his values or conduct. It doesn't mean you have to be a personal friend.

We need to be careful to show respect for all people. Regardless of his personality, a guy is worthy of reverence by the simple fact that he is God's creation. Besides, your respect is an extremely powerful influence and invitation for a guy to act mature.

There are times when the way a guy acts just sort of invites a verbal smack-down, don't you think? Or at least a snub. But if you do that, it compels the guy to keep up his defenses. That means you may never see the real guy. On the other hand, when you're kind and you resist the temptation to make sarcastic retorts and put-downs, you provide an environment where a guy will feel comfortable to be real. Often your casual acceptance is all that's needed to disarm a cocky guy.

It's majorly important to know the *real* guy. That's what protects you from being deceived. That's how you learn whether or not you want to become *better* acquainted with him.

That's also how *he* discovers if he wants to know *you* better! If a guy starts to show his true personality and a girl teases him, she'll get checked off his list fast. It's an old law that you don't shoot an unarmed man. Don't attack when his defenses are down.

> Putting down a guy when he's being real tells the guy that you are not a safe person to be around and that you can't be trusted.

So whether or not you like a guy's personality, in the long run it pays to be kind and nonjudgmental. Either way then, you end up a winner.

You can spot a scheming *girl* a mile away, right? Well, guys can zero in on a jerk too. They have a special form of male communication, a knack for understanding each other. Guys can tell when another guy is being phony with a girl. That can be to your benefit. If your brother or a brother-type friend warns you about some guy that you're interested in or have a crush on, you might want to listen to him. He may be trying to prevent you from being hurt. Guys really *can* detect other guys' intentions. It's nice to be protected by caring guys.

Still, you need to pray for discernment in order to avoid being bamboozled. A lot depends on the guy who's warning you. He may indeed have your best interests at heart *or* he may have his *own* interests in mind!

Dan and Kyle both had a crush on Ashley. She was friends with both of them but had a special relationship with Kyle. Unfortunately, when

Dan started telling Ashley stories about Kyle, she believed him. Dan came across as if he was looking out for Ashley, but his intentions were anything but noble.

Now here's the weird part. When Kyle discovered his friend was sabotaging his relationship with Ashley, he was angry with him. But he was *more* offended with Ashley for believing Dan. Kyle had been completely loyal to her and was deeply hurt that she would so easily believe stuff that another person said about him. His hurt turned to disgust, then to disillusionment and finally to disinterest. It will take prayer for their friendship to be restored.

By reflecting on the quality of the relationship she'd had with Kyle up to that point, considering his character and using a bit of discernment, Ashley could have avoided falling into Dan's trap.

Preppy, Mr. Muscles, gangsta, class clown, school jock . . . when we're looking at different types of guys, we have to learn to look past their exteriors. There's a lot more to them than what we see on the outside. Beneath each surface is a real guy, and there are reasons for the image he portrays.

Different Stages

At the same time you're trying to figure out what type of person a guy is, you also need to understand what stage he's in! What do I mean by *stage?* Guys go through a wide range of attitudes toward females. Their ideas about girls change in a variety of ways as they grow up. Preschool, elementary school, middle school, high school and college-age guys all have drastically different outlooks toward females. They experience several mental and emotional adjustments before reaching the age when they begin looking for a wife.

[
It's much easier to know what to expect from a guy
if you have some idea of what stage he's in.
]

Since they don't all go through the same stage at exactly the same age, it's a little tricky; but here's an overview of those stages as I've seen them. Let's consider them chronologically.

Friends

When boys are very young, they don't care whether they play with boys or girls. They just want to play, period. And they want to be friends. It's a sweet time. They talk and play with boys *and* girls as sincerely as a little person can. This usually lasts until about kindergarten.

Once they start school, they also begin their playground education, which is passed on to them by older students. One of those hard-learned lessons is that boys and girls are different. If you play with girls, you're gonna get teased. Boys quickly learn that being teased isn't fun, so they begin to withdraw from girls at this stage. Since boys value friendships, some boys simply become more discreet about *when* they play with girls.

Cooties

By the time boys are in about first or second grade, Barbies® and things pink, lavender or sparkly just don't appeal to them. They've been around other boys enough to discover the fun of boisterous activities and decide that's the camp with which they want to identify. To justify this, boys make the break by deciding girls have cooties. (Of course it's fairly mutual because this happens around the same time that girls are deciding that boys have germs.)

Bachelors Forever

With cooties and germs setting the boundaries, boys go through the next couple of years with NO GIRLS ALLOWED signs posted on their clubhouses and on their attitudes. Sometimes boys direct teasing toward girls. They are reinforcing the distance between them and girls. They are also barricading themselves from the teasing they receive *from* girls. At this stage, boys earnestly make pacts among themselves that they'll be bachelors forever. And they mean it!

Crushes

Pssst, here's a bonus secret! This is *really* the inside scoop, so don't tell anyone . . . but . . . in the midst of *any* of these stages, guys can become traitors to the code. One guy confided to me that all guys go through this but they'll never admit it to each other. After all, there's that bachelors forever pact, right? Alas, it's an unspoken angst they must suffer alone—having a secret crush on a female!

Camp counselors, teachers, a friend's older sister—even girls their own age—can all be targets for a boy's secret adoration. Sometimes girls catch on, but others never know.

As an older girl, if you think you're the recipient of a boy's undying affections, be flattered but don't tease or flirt. His feelings can be so easily hurt. You represent the female of the species to this boy. Let him know that girls are approachable. It will give him sweet memories and build a healthy base for his overall attitude toward girls.

Peter Pan

Things start changing around fourth or fifth grade. Among the girls, that is. They begin going through puberty. Thoughts about guys having germs begin to fade and are replaced with daydreams of Prince Charming.

> Unfortunately, a fourth or fifth grade Prince Charming is still living the life of Peter Pan.

Not only is he not ready to grow up, he's still busy refining and perfecting the art of being a boy. That can mean anything from planning the perfect scare tactic against his sister to mastering tricks on a skateboard.

Embarrassed

That "little boy" streak in guys doesn't want to face or deal with the changes they see in their female counterparts. They are used to seeing girls in a different light. Now they're witnessing you turn into young ladies. When they see the front of your blouse changing shape, that's something they need to get used to. Boys don't automatically think it's great. They go through a stage of feeling embarrassed. They're not keeping pace with you physically.

Curious

This is *definitely* not the time to put boys down. They might seem dorky or immature to girls right now, but guys will, in time, have their growth spurts too. When they do, that boy you were looking down on will likely be looking down on you, with either good or bad memories of how you treated him earlier.

Though they're not ready to fulfill their Prince Charming roles, this is a time when boys are more open to friendships with girls again. They're curious. They want to dare to approach girls without feeling overwhelmed. They're not yet ready to pursue. Girls need to keep their "nesting instincts" in check and be content with building friendships with guys again. This is the ideal age for a girl to begin keeping a little mystery about herself!

Struggles

From here the stages become even more difficult to define by age or school grade. Guys go through a time of inward struggle as they come to grips with growing up. The social order among their peers is shifting. They struggle with the awakening of their own sexuality and the temptations that accompany it. The idea of being friends with girls again is becoming increasingly attractive.

Attracted

Male hormones are kicking in. Girls become an appealing topic of conversation. *Cooties? Don't you mean cuties?* The guys want to be around you, get to know you and spend time with you. They think about girls nearly 24/7. And, in some respects, they'll start to pursue now. But, and pardon the expression but this is a *big* but, the guys are *not* ready or mature enough for making relationship commitments.

When a guy has a steady girlfriend around this time, sometimes it's because he feels pressured into it. Other guys devote themselves to a girl because she's truly special to him. But even then, trust me, *he's not* thinking about marriage! Guys are pretty enthusiastic about girls now, but they still haven't left their Peter Pan days behind. (More about this in Secret No. 7.)

Entertainment

This is a very important stage. More is at stake. Boys have now become men, physically. Their bodies are ready and *willing* to reproduce. A better word might even be *demanding!*

Remember the huggy homecoming the girls gave Myles in the chapter on keeping mystery? Can you now see why all those hugs were more stimulation than Myles should have had to deal with? Have mercy on the guys!

> Guys today are tested to the limit, being exposed to so much female nudity while still being expected to keep their demanding bodies under control.

At this stage, girls who flirt and flaunt their bodies are asking for trouble; they become a form of entertainment for many guys. (Those same girls feel puzzled and hurt because the guys aren't willing to make a commitment.)

Guys at this stage aren't marriage-minded. They're looking for fun, adventure and entertainment. And the quality guys are also *trying* to focus on building their futures. They're not thinking of settling down.

> As much as you might yearn to hear a guy say that you're the one for him, it is not to your advantage to seduce a guy into making a commitment.

Premature promises of devotion can lead to events that painfully affect the rest of your life.

Guys haven't had time to prepare for a career yet. They're not emotionally or financially ready for marriage. At this stage, for everyone's protection, relationships between guys and girls should be carefully submitted to parents and the Lord.

Friends

As guys mature, they look for girls who won't play games with their emotions. They want girl *friends* whom they can trust and be comfortable around. (Just remember to keep some mystery!) They want solid friendships built on quality values and respect. Yes, their hormones are still screaming for attention, but they're also thinking about their futures. They are on the verge of the next stage.

Pursuit

Believe it or not, there really *does* come a time when a guy actually thinks about marriage and finding a wife! At this stage, guys closely consider what kind of a wife and mother a girl will be. (They pay attention to those qualities in a girl long before this, but until this stage, it doesn't influence them as much in their friendships with females.) When a guy believes he's found that quality girl, the pursuit is on!

There is quite a long time between the Peter Pan stage and the

Pursuit stage, but the wait is important—and worth it—because it gives you the time needed to develop *your* character and become a quality woman of God. But finally, when guys are eager to seriously focus on a relationship, being properly pursued can be pretty wonderful.

> With all this variety in guys and their attitudes toward girls, you can see why it's a waste of time trying to change your personality to please a certain guy!

Why bother? There are bound to be guys who like the real you. Remember, it's by your being real that guys feel invited to be real too!

The only person you need to consider changing for is the Lord. That's very liberating. And there's something even more wonderful about this. By his grace, God makes the needed changes *in* you as you pray, study your Bible and obey. As you conform to his design, you'll become the right kind of girl for the right guy, who has *also* been cooperating with the Lord's changing grace!

When you take into consideration these differences in guys, you'll have a more accurate picture of what each guy is really like. Then you can adjust your expectations. The guys will be *so* relieved! And, along the way, you'll probably discover that guys are even more delightful than you thought.

Secret No. 5

Guys vs. Girls

Guys feel they can't talk to you about this, but here's a secret that's vitally important to them: guys don't like competitive guy-vs.-girl contests.

Imagine how you'd feel if you were put into a position where, no matter what you did, you were guaranteed to lose, every time. Would you feel frustrated? angry? discouraged? bitter? Might you feel like giving up? Guys are overloaded with these kinds of feelings every time they're put into guys-vs.-girls circumstances. They feel as though it's automatically a lose-lose situation. On one hand, when guys win a contest, they're put in a male chauvinist category. If they lose, they're humiliated and their male egos are bruised.

> [No matter what the outcome of a
> particular competition, even when the
> guys "win," they ultimately lose.]

Merely trying to tell girls they don't want to be part of this rivalry puts guys at a disadvantage. If they attempt to decline a challenge, they get razzed for being sissies. If they try explaining that they don't like the idea of overpowering girls and they don't want to accidentally injure them, they're blasted for being sexist. It's no wonder guys feel they can't discuss this with you.

There are lots of gender competitions these days, but I've rarely seen a guy initiate any of them. Challenges to outdo males are mostly generated by feminists and those who have jumped on the politically correct bandwagon. Other adults promote these contests too but with innocent intentions or certainly without understanding the consequences. These influences have taught girls a nyah-nyah attitude toward guys.

There's a lot of laughing over anti-boy antics, but the guys aren't laughing. If it were just an occasional gentle poke, it might be easier to see the humor, but guys are fed a steady diet of anti-guy stuff from the time they're small.

Competition locks girls into a no-win situation as well. If the girls win the contest, it forfeits the openness the guys may have felt with them. If they lose, girls usually feel some degree of humiliation, resentment or bitterness. At the least, sarcastic comments begin flying from both sides. (Well, don't they?)

Competition, by its very nature, produces a striving between opponents. Obviously, in order for there to be a winner, someone must be the loser. One is triumphant, the other defeated. One is superior, the other inferior. The winner exalts at the other's expense.

What benefit is there for either guys or girls? There's nothing relationship-friendly about words like striving and opponent. To strive against someone is to make him your adversary, your enemy. To oppose someone is to hinder his progress.

It's sort of like two magnets. When each is turned in the correct direction, the attraction between them is so strong they can hardly be kept apart. Turn one magnet in the opposite direction, however, and they repel each other. It's impossible for them to be put together; one pushes the other away.

That's not exactly an ideal environment for bonding with guys, is it? If your goal is to prove that you're better than guys, how will that work when you want to attract one? Or when guys want to woo you? How can men and women be in love with and serve each other if they're fighting to prove who's superior? Amos 3:3 asks, "Do two walk together unless they have agreed to do so?"

There are no winners in guys vs. girls contests

There are no winners in guys vs. girls contests, yet the battle of the sexes has been going on for ages. It has heated up significantly in the last thirty to forty years. Now it's actually promoted! And adult females are leading the charge. The feminist movement is such a touchy subject, I wish I didn't have to bring it up; but you're directly affected, so it's not fair to you to overlook it.

> [Young people today are the victims of this
> females-against-males mind-set.]

You have had no say in the matter. If you're younger than thirty-five, you have known no other environment. For girls, competing with guys is portrayed as perfectly normal. Out-doing guys is encouraged and touted as praiseworthy. The truth is, you're being raised in a male-bashing society. And it doesn't hurt only guys; it's just as harmful to girls!

How and why did this happen? In what way does our society bash males? And how does it hurt us females? Whoa! Let's take these questions one at a time.

How and why did our culture become a male-bashing society?

Women's rights is a complex subject, but basically, our culture was oppressive and unfair to women on some issues and definitely needed to change.

(It's important to understand that when women are mistreated by men, it is not because they are men, it's because people are sinners! *Females* mistreat females too. Ask any girl in middle school if this isn't true! You don't have to be very old to know how nastily girls can treat each other, right? Whether it's men or women, the problem is the same. It's not gender—it's sin.)

For varying reasons, certain women took it upon themselves to change our society. They wanted equal rights—meaning equal with men. The result is the feminist movement.

Let's give them the benefit of the doubt. Let's say those women genuinely wanted to bring about positive change. Are good intentions enough? We have an example of the results of good intentions in the Bible in the book of Judges. Throughout that book, the Israelites were often without leaders, so "every man did that which was right in his own eyes" (Judges 17:6, KJV). You'll want to read the passage to get the whole picture. You'll see that "every man" included women, and you'll also see that the results were disastrous. Outrageous decisions were made and innocent people suffered.

It's no different today. No matter how earnest our efforts, when relying only on our own judgment, we are unable to make wise decisions. Man's vision is limited while God's is long-range. People try their own solutions, but God has set forth principles that work. And God makes his wisdom available to all who are willing to humble themselves to receive it (James 1:5-7).

Like the people in the book of Judges, the women spearheading the feminist movement went about things in a way that was right in their own eyes. They overlooked the root problem of sin and instead attacked men as a gender. The result?

> Instead of having a healthier society, we have one
> that is simply warped in a different direction.
> Now we have a male-bashing society.

In what way does our society bash males?

You begin hearing the message while you're very young. Cartoons and many children's books portray the father as a bumbling idiot, always making mistakes and getting himself and his family into trouble. Mama is the problem solver; she bails him out.

TV sitcoms send the same message: dads are immature, foolish, irresponsible, unreliable and incapable, while moms are smart, levelheaded, trustworthy and *they* can do *any*thing! Basically (these messages tell us), women straighten out all the stuff that men goof up.

You might know how it feels to be nagged. Can you imagine how it is for guys to grow up with the constant message that they don't measure up?

> Today's men have been raised with the "loser" label
> and many accept it without question.

They not only live up to, or rather, *down* to this new portrayal of males, but many can be found agreeing with it. Male scriptwriters and advertising copy writers actually brainstorm to come up with clever ways to mock and put down their fellowman, in the name of humor—the more hilarious the better.

I recently watched a TV commercial that showed a guy at the kitchen sink, a dish towel flung over his shoulder. I don't remember the point of the ad or the product, but I do remember the expression on the wife's face. We viewers were supposed to think it was funny too. The chagrined husband was the butt of the mocking advertisement, and the wife was most certainly in triumph mode.

I used to wonder why guys put up with that kind of treatment. But once I realized their no-win choices, their passive response made sense. It goes right back to their dislike for guys vs. girls battles. Fighting back is just another losing option.

When guys endure belittling treatment, it's often interpreted as being wimpy. In reality, the ability to suffer in silence is one of the noble strengths of men. But guys have their limits, and it's a good idea for us ladies to take that to heart.

Guys have one strategy that they do use. They simply remove themselves from the presence of the abuse. That can mean a guy's leaving a wife he has been married to for many years. It's usually a shock to the wife because her husband tolerated her tirades for such a long time before he cut out. Younger guys, who catch on, distance themselves from girls like this before they reach the altar. That's not a winning stance for girls either.

One day I received an e-mail that listed questions given to elementary school children about their mothers, along with the kids' answers. When asked: *Who's the boss at your house?* one youngster replied, "Mom doesn't want to be boss, but she has to because dad's such a goofball." The kids' remarks were intended to make us smile, but this child's response revealed that he was growing up without admiration or respect for his dad. His dad quite likely grew up feeling like a loser. And the cycle continues as this boy learns the same defeatist outlook from his role-model dad.

You deserve to know that it hasn't always been like this. Before the 1960s, children's books such as those in the *Little House on the Prairie* set and TV programs like *Father Knows Best* portrayed the father as a wise leader and protective head of the home. The dad was the one whom the rest of the family members revered and looked to for provision, guidance and help.

People mock and call those books and programs ridiculously

outdated, but they model the role that the Lord designed for men. The attitude that traditional families are old-fashioned and no longer relevant is an example of people doing and thinking, "what is right in their own eyes." It shows how far those who laugh have strayed from God's Word. Fashions and lifestyles come and go, but God is always current! His Word will never be outdated. In fact, it's the only thing that *won't* pass away (Matthew 24:35; 1 Corinthians 7:31)!

Don't believe it when you hear that *Leave It to Beaver* families never existed. We are told this by people who want to justify the breakdown of the family unit as God ordained it. There are no perfect people so it's impossible for a family to be flawless, but *Father Knows Best* families not only *did* exist, they *still do*! And God wants more of them.

> God wants healthy families
> as he created them to be.

They include a father who lovingly leads his family, his wife who supports and respects him, and obedient children (Malachi 2:15; Ephesians 5:22, 23; 6:1-4).

But how can families be healthy and how can guys become good leaders if, from the time they are little boys, guys live in a male-bashing environment where they are no longer looked upon as heroes, but as the laughingstock and butt of jokes?

Here's what I have observed: from the time boys are born, they are compared with girls. Because they develop in different ways than girls and not at the same rate, those comparisons are unreasonable and illogical.

The differences are not taken into consideration in most schools, so boys receive their education generally believing they don't measure up. You'd never guess this, passing guys in the hall, would you? They're very good at ignoring or hiding pain.

With those daily messages of defeat, many boys who are actually bright lose heart and withdraw to worlds they know they *can* conquer—on video and computer screens, for example. Instead of growing up with a love for learning, they pass from grade to grade, merely enduring school. Subconsciously they reason: *If school stinks, and school is the pathway to my future, then my future must stink too.* Their activities and the way they spend their time reflect their loss of hope and vision.

Besides academics, boys find themselves forced into circumstances where they must compete further with girls who are placed in their midst for sport activities. In the past several years, this has been happening more and more. Girls now participate in contact sports such as wrestling, making teams mixed-gender.

Legislation can't change a guy's heart

The girls may have their place on the team but legislation can't change the heart of a guy. Guys don't really want to be pitted against girls. Ask any young man on a wrestling team how he *really* feels about having a female opponent.

> I've seen the emotional torment and guilt that
> guys go through in trying to overcome their
> God-given reluctance to overpower a girl.

(Not to mention how they freak out at the idea of being forced to have their hands all over her body).

One of our sons went through this. After much *inner* wrestling, he decided to forfeit a wrestling match rather than go against his female opponent. His teammates, some of whom were state qualifiers, admitted they would have done the same thing. That inner objection is programmed into guys' hearts by the Lord who designed men to protect women (1 Samuel 30:1-19; Ephesians 5:25, 28). This was definitely one of those no-win situations for our son. But I was proud of his decision; he showed winning character.

The feminist movement insists that girls be treated "equal" with boys in all areas. Guys, on the other hand, are not comfortable trying to live equal with girls in all areas of identity that girls possess. When guys do enter that domain, it is obvious that it's not normal, even though our culture is trying desperately to convince you that homosexuality is simply an alternate lifestyle.

The message of equality is not as across-the-board as we are led to believe. There's quite a bit of hypocrisy mixed in. With all the new rights for girls, certain social rules haven't changed. Even though girls are allowed to mock boys and are encouraged to compete with them on every level, modern etiquette still says boys can't hit girls. I'm glad that rule hasn't changed, but it shows how feminism-style equality is lopsided.

Equality definitely stops short in the area of dress (no pun intended). If feminists are so eager to be treated the same as men, why, with every passing year of the movement, have women become more brazen in their conduct and more provocative in their attire? It's a very mixed message. Women not only emphasize the female-ness of their bodies by exposing them, they make no apologies for it, and they use this sex difference for exploiting men. Can you see the hypocrisy?

It's more than hypocritical. Immodesty is insulting and degrading to men. It reveals a notable lack of respect for men as creatures whom God created after his own image. And it's grossly unfair. Women know that exposed flesh is intimidating and disturbing to men. Using our God-given influence of sexuality as a weapon against men is a last straw insult toward men and ultimately toward God. *That* is a very scary position for women to put themselves in.

How does living in a male-bashing society hurt us females?

The most sobering drawback from putting down guys is that it puts us in trouble with God. The main issue isn't friction between guys and girls; it's an issue of God's creation rebelling against *him*. Women and girls who insist on being treated the same as men are, in reality, not shaking their angry fists in the faces of men, but of God.

It was God's idea to create two distinct sexes! Not one, two.

> God deliberately, on purpose, wholeheartedly
> and *perfectly* made a distinction between men
> and women. He ordained different purposes
> and roles for men and women.

"And," in God's own words, "it was very good" (Genesis 1:31).

The militant feminists are fighting hard to neutralize these differences. Doing what is right in their own eyes, they're trying to erase distinctions between men and women. Now, is that silly or what? Actually, it's not silly, it's sad. God loves those women. He sees their hurt and frustration, but their ways don't work.

Their methods of obtaining "equality" are misguided. In the first place, they're fighting God. When God says something, that's the way it is. He made men *and* women. Second, trying to erase gender can't guarantee fair treatment. That's attacking the wrong problem; it isn't gender, it's sin. In promoting unisex, the militant feminists have only caused a horrible confusion among men and women as to their roles.

Because their identity as males has been stolen from them and shamed out of them by the feminist movement, guys are left wondering what makes them distinctly male. Perplexed as to their identity, they reason, *When it comes to my sex, I guess I can choose.* Rather than facing the ridicule and rejection of females, many are choosing the acceptance of other males.

That I'm-just-as-good-as-the-guys attitude in women and girls is the same defiance that Satan demonstrated toward God. It got him thrown out of Heaven (Isaiah 14:12-14; Luke 10:18; Revelation 12:7-9). Rebellion is very devilish. God says "rebellion is as bad as the sin of witchcraft" (1 Samuel 15:23, NLT).

Have you noticed how witchcraft is becoming increasingly common? I have seen displays of books and magazines on witchcraft specifically designed for teen girls. Don't even pick them up! Ouija® boards, tarot cards, wicca, séances, horror movies and certain video games and music—it's all a hellish plan to destroy you.

Oh yes, you *can* leave them alone! After learning that reading her horoscope was delving into witchcraft, Stephanie stopped reading it. Sometimes she was tempted with thoughts like, *Well, I don't really believe it* and *Once isn't gonna hurt.* (All the devil needs is a little opening to get his foot in the door of your life.) But Stephanie rejected those temptations and she has stayed true to her decision to this day. You can too!

[
Do you think it's significant that witchcraft is developing parallel with the feminist movement?
]

Let's stop here for a minute and take a tally. What other social phenomena have grown in prominence at the same time as the militant feminist movement? Sex outside of marriage. Teen pregnancy. Abortion. Homosexuality. Even though people's views have changed on these issues, God's standards for our sexuality have not changed. Take a few minutes and look up these passages: Romans 1:21-27; 1 Corinthians 6:9, 10; Ephesians 5:3; 1 Thessalonians 4:3-5. Do you think there's a connection between the rise of feminism, wicca and the downward spiral of these sexual sins? Absolutely!

As a girl, can you see how a male-bashing society hurts you? When we put guys down, we're undermining our own welfare. Either directly or indirectly, all females suffer the consequences!

Did you know that it is a sign of God's judgment when women dominate a culture? You can read about it in Isaiah 3. Other signs of his displeasure are listed there too, one being youth that are intimidating and rebellious. But the even more notable sign is that male leadership is removed!

So when men are missing from leadership roles, and mostly women are in charge, it's a sign that God is not pleased? Isaiah 3 might be a good chapter to read and discuss with your parents.

If trying to be just like guys is rebellion, where does that leave us girls? Are we second-class citizens? God absolutely loves the idea of females! He declared his idea "very good," remember? You are his very good idea! (God isn't the only one who loves the idea of females. Guys do too; they're delighted with the differences!)

> Being a female doesn't make you less important. It makes you distinct. God isn't calling you to compete with guys. He's calling you to be the very best you that *you* can be.

Comparisons don't work. It's illogical to compare yourself to a guy. Is a peach inferior because it doesn't look or taste like an apple? Check this out. In an October 1999 report from the Society for Women's Health Research: "Researchers used to think of women as 'little men,' but in the past ten years, science has uncovered biological and physiological gender differences in virtually every organ in the human body." (Taken from "Maybe Not Sugar & Spice, But Women Are Very Different When It Comes To Biology," Society for Women's Health Research). Isn't that awesome? We are gloriously unique!

The whole concept of competing with guys doesn't make sense either. When we take on the role of a guy, we are taking a position that God hasn't given us and trying to accomplish a task that he hasn't assigned to us. That doesn't sound like a good formula for success, does it? Instead of trying to compete with guys, why not celebrate *your* gender, *your* femininity, and enjoy the differences of roles? The way for us females to rise to our full potential is by embracing who we are.

It's your motive!

God is looking at *motives*. Guys pick up on motives too! In the chapter on guys' ideas about beauty, you read about two girls who were beautiful, humble and loved to have fun (swinging from a tree rope, riding horses, etc.). If those girls had been engaged in those activities with the sole purpose of trying to outdo the guys—swing farther, ride faster—it would have put a whole different spin on the way the guys saw those girls. That difference would have been because of the girls' motives. It would have had nothing to do with what they were doing.

If you want to outdo guys, ask yourself why. *Why is it important for me to beat a guy?* Isn't the bottom line to prove you're better? Then what? Where does gloating over a defeated guy get you? If you follow that line of thinking, you'll see that the result is a lonely and sad place to end. When a girl aligns herself to competitively take the same role as a guy, she's like that turned-around magnet—she repels. There can't be a winning situation when girls and guys try to put each other down.

God is certainly not saying that we females can't do many of the same things that guys do. Scores of activities, ministries and responsibilities can be performed just as well by girls as by guys. But God hasn't called us to strife.

The girls-vs.-guys mentality, the competition, the battles between the sexes all need to stop.

> God created us to work together as a team. He gave men and women roles that *complement* each other!

When we're jockeying with guys for position, we're being counterproductive to the plans of God. We may be praying, "Thy kingdom come, thy will be done," but in essence we're hindering God's will. We're disobeying God. That grieves him.

Males and females alike have vastly underestimated the importance that God places on our getting along with one another. The Bible is full of Scriptures showing the enormous priority that God places on harmony and unity among his people (see Psalm 133; John 13:34; 17:21; Galatians 5:13-15; Ephesians 4:1-3; 5:1, 2; Philippians 2:2-7; 1 Timothy 5:1, 2, for example). It's not acceptable to God when guys treat girls as second-class citizens, and it's not all right with God for young ladies to degrade guys.

I have never seen anything in God's Word that encourages competition between the sexes. He commands us to love one another. Our heavenly Father has given us a multitude of Scriptures about how we are to treat one another, and he left no room for guy-girl bashing.

God has also given guideline Scriptures for our roles. Among them are Genesis 3:16-19; Proverbs 31:10-31; 1 Corinthians 11:3; Ephesians 5:21-33; 6:1-4; Colossians 3:18-21; 1 Timothy 3:1-12; Titus 2:1-8; and 1 Peter 3:1-9. Men do not attain their place in society by trying to hold women back. Women do not gain their place in society by displacing men. It's not necessary to elbow a guy out of your way. God's plan is peaceful and it involves both sexes. He is not a God of confusion (1 Corinthians 14:33).

Everyone has a personal destiny laid out for him or her by the master creator. You don't have to fight for your place because God has already prepared—and is holding it—just for you (Ephesians 2:10). If there is any fighting necessary, God will fight for you. Vindication—and even promotion—comes from him (Romans 12:16-21; Psalm 75:6, 7, KJV)!

Forget guys for a minute and think about Jesus. Have you been a hindrance to his prayers for unity by striving for superiority over guys? If you need to, ask his forgiveness for that. Tell the Lord you want to be a blessing to his kingdom, not a hindrance. Let him know you're done with fighting and that you're willing to trust him to lead you into your destiny. Ask him to make you a team player and to fill your heart with peace and a supportive attitude toward guys. This is the first step toward finding your wonderfully fulfilling place on this planet.

Now you're ready to think about guys again! And, oh boy, you have no idea how glad guys will be to have your *support!*

A great place to begin is in your own home. You can practice by showing an encouraging attitude toward your dad. Let him know you appreciate all he does for you. Thank him for specific things. Treat him with respect. Ask his advice.

If you have a difference of opinion, rather than letting your feelings explode, calmly ask your dad if you may explain how you feel. Then share from your heart rationally. There's a bottom-line issue going on here. Guys and girls are different. Males tend to be rational thinkers and women tend to respond emotionally. It will be easier for your dad to "hear" you if you make an effort to talk his language.

Ask your dad about *his* day. Listen to him. Is there anything you can be praying about for him? Become an intercessor for your dad. God has called men to be the leaders of their homes. That makes them the primary target of the enemy, Satan. God has called women to be suitable helpers for men (Genesis 2:18; 3:16). Be your dad's helper by standing in the gap through prayer. It's great practice for being the support that your future husband will need. Do you have any idea how it can strengthen your dad when he sees your eyes glisten with admiration for him? Try it, and see if you don't benefit as well!

Your next project of support should still be in your own household—your brother(s)! If he's older, apply the same things for him as for your dad. You could have a huge healing influence in your brother's life if you begin supporting and encouraging him. Most brothers would love to have a sister with whom they feel comfortable to bounce off thoughts about girls. (You may be tempted to think it's funny but don't you *dare* tell your friends anything that your brother confides in you!)

[Guys want to understand girls.]

Your respect and trustworthiness will teach him volumes. Be one of his best friends.

If you have a pesky little brother(s), wow, do you ever have clout here! You're in a powerful position to mold his attitudes toward females for the rest of his life. His antics may drive you nuts, but that's a little boy's way of getting attention from a female. Lay some great foundations in his mischievous little heart by resisting the temptation to put him in his place. Speak positively to him. Have fun with him; let him know you enjoy him. When he's scared, let him know that it's OK to be afraid. If he cries, assure him that guys cry—Jesus did, even when he was a grown man! Let your little brother know that you see him as a hero-in-the-making.

And last, but definitely not least, support the other guys in your life. At school, church, work, all guys desperately want to achieve their God-ordained roles.

> Guys need affirmation as the worthwhile men
> God created them to be.

Allow a guy to make mistakes without getting in his face and saying, "I told you so." Call a halt to the friction stuff and declare peace. Competitions can be fun, but if the sides involve guys vs. girls, be bold in suggesting that the teams be mixed.

Guys deserve our respect and as females it's definitely to our advantage to give it. That means networking *with* them instead of rising up against them. Have you any idea how valuable that can make you to a guy? Talk about magnetic attraction!

Secret No. 6

Guys Are Allergic to Silliness

Remember when you were little? The days when guys had germs and girls had cooties? You're probably breathing a sigh of relief that those days are but a dim memory now. The guys are glad too. They're starting to enjoy the idea of being around girls. In fact, most of them are waaaay past just *starting* to like the idea!

It's really more like this: picture a bunch of guys standing around joking among themselves. Then some girls come into view. This causes a hotties alert! All heads swivel in the direction of the young ladies and the conversation instantly changes . . . or drops off completely. Whatever the guys were laughing about is forgotten. Something more interesting has riveted their attention. Chicks!

The guys' mannerisms switch from jovial to cool, and their conversation turns to strategizing, mapping out a plan for approaching and meeting those girls.

Yes, it's times like that when it's fun to be a female! And, come on now . . . admit it . . . the guys are on your radar screens too, right? You'd like to meet them. Don't tell me you're not doing your *own* plotting. This is another female talking to you; I've been where you are. But here's the good part: I live in the world of guys now. I've discovered another valuable secret.

As much as they are fascinated by your presence . . .

There *is* something that will make the guys draw back like the parting of the Red Sea. That's when girls start acting silly.

Guys don't like being around girls' silliness. It causes flashbacks to the cooties days. And stirs up a lot of other stuff too.

When the guys are looking (or at least you think they *might* be)— and you're looking too (but you don't want to *look* like you're looking, but you still want them to notice), this is *not* the time to act silly!

I know that's a tough pill to swallow. Wanting guys' attention is a totally natural female thing. How else can you be sure guys are gonna notice if you're not doing something *notice*able?

You can relax. Guys are visual. They have no problem spotting girls in the vicinity. Not only can they spot you, guys can do it without your knowing. They enjoy being able to observe for a while, undetected. Acting silly *will* get their attention too, but it sure doesn't get their admiration.

Guys' "allergies" to girls' silliness go way back to the "eeuuw, cooties" days. That Dennis-the-Menace attitude is a standard little-boy response. At that age, they want nothing to do with girls dressing their kittens like dolls or having tea parties—activities which, of course, we girls know aren't at *all* silly! But we outgrew that era. And so did the guys; they don't want to go back there.

What translates as silliness to guys now? It usually occurs when girls are in groups glancing at guys, whispering, giggling, laughing loudly, squealing, shrieking, stumbling around, etc. It definitely gets their attention, but it's a big turnoff and sends guys in the opposite direction—sometimes permanently.

At your age, guys have gladly renounced their bachelors forever pledge. They find themselves wondering why they ever considered such a pact. But being around girls who act silly is embarrassing to them and gives them pause to rethink the benefits of being a bachelor. Their initial fascination comes to an abrupt halt and the guys make a U-turn.

Please understand . . .

[
I'm not saying to quit having girl fun.
I'm saying it's best saved for slumber parties
and girls-only settings.
]

Part of the fun of being a girl is in reserving that right for private—and exclusive—get-togethers of the sisterhood. You know, those chick gatherings where you let down your hair . . . paint your toenails, whisper, giggle, pluck your brows, talk about guys, try new hairdos, chew bubble gum, get s'mores in your braces, shriek with laughter . . . But when you leave that girls-only place, leave your girls-only conduct there too.

Rest assured, guys definitely have their own form of silliness. Do they ever! Being the only female presence in our family, and being vastly outnumbered when our sons have guests, I've been privy to the kind of humor that guys reserve for all-male bonding. There have been times when I *so* didn't want to be in the midst of their guy humor. I would have preferred to never learn about it.

No, I don't mean it's X-rated. The stuff that guys think is funny . . . it's just . . . well . . . interesting. As a female, I guess I'd label a lot of their humor as just plain gross. Need I say more? Ladies, you can live your lives quite nicely without ever being exposed to it. But, since I do get exposed to it, I'll admit that the guys endear themselves to me all the more by the reverence they show toward girls in refraining from their normally gross manner of silliness around them. Guys are right; it does need to stay among the males. Keep your silliness among yourselves as well.

Poise Pays

This issue goes back to what guys find beautiful about girls. It's really just practical. Let's review. The first thing guys notice is your appearance, and the second thing is your conduct. A guy doesn't want to picture himself out in the community with a female who acts foolish. Guys admire girls who conduct themselves with poise in public.

Not many guys are enamored by girls who try to be comediennes. (That doesn't rule out all guys though; remember they're not all alike.) If you have a knack for comedy, ask the Lord to teach you how to use this gift without being foolish. You can be a huge blessing using humor creatively.

Often though, girls' being silly is a ploy to get attention. (I say this gently.) But it's sort of a waste of effort. Guys *want* to give girls attention anyway. It's just that they want to choose to whom and when to give it. Girls' vying for guys' attention by acting silly can be a control/competition issue. If you're in control, the guys are not going to fight you for it. (It's that guys-vs.-girls secret.) And if you're calling the shots by pursuing their attention, you're not a challenge. (It's that mystery secret.)

So silliness is out. But what is in? If we go back to that same scene—a bunch of guys spotting a group of girls—what will make those swiveled heads stay turned in the direction of the girls because of admiration?

The guys themselves give clues. When they spot you, they drop their horsing around. Outwardly, they appear calm and casual. And occupied. What they do is determined by the setting. If they're outdoors, they might engage in some easy sport like playing catch. At the mall, they may begin peering in a shop window. However they occupy themselves, they manage to do it while keeping the girls in their sights.

The same plan works well for girls too. Your peaceful and relaxed demeanor (calm and casual) is attractive to guys.

> If you're occupied as well, it sends the message that you have a life, that you're not holding your breath waiting for the guys to give you attention.

Feel free to enjoy yourselves, but without causing a scene.

Perhaps it sounds a bit conniving to call this a plan. In reality, it's a short lesson in social etiquette. There's nothing devious about that. There are charm schools and courses that exist for the sole purpose of teaching proper demeanor and deportment. It's even being taught at MIT, the Massachusetts Institute of Technology, and is a very popular course. Check out http://web.mit.edu/slp/charm/geninfo.html.

In the Bible, Esther spent an entire year going through "charm and beauty school" in preparation for meeting the king. It was worth her effort. She became the king's wife. Studying proper grooming and etiquette showed wisdom, and it was God who orchestrated the whole plan!

You're not being phony when you practice appealing behavior. Even if it doesn't feel natural at first, any young lady can learn manners and social graces.

When she was growing up, Bobbi could hold her own against most guys. She was better at throwing a baseball and better at shooting guns. She wouldn't back down from a fight either. A skinny, scrappy girl with a short haircut, Bobbi saw herself as the son her father wanted. She desperately yearned for his approval.

When she was sent to live with an aunt, Bobbi was in for a shock. There she was allowed to wear only dresses and was not permitted to whistle. "You talk too loud," she was told, "and walk too loud. Walk softly, sit gracefully."

"I realize now that I needed those extreme opposite influences to bring balance into my life," Bobbi says. Today she is a beautiful, elegant and accomplished woman who, one would never guess, is still an expert marksman.

Bobbi didn't need to unlearn behavior as much as she needed to learn *more*—what is appropriate for what occasion or circumstance. She'll be the first one to tell you that competing with guys doesn't work in a marriage.

[Learning poise needn't be complicated.
Sometimes it's as simple as remaining quiet.]

While reading her Bible one day, Olivia was intrigued by a particular verse. "Even a fool is thought wise if he keeps silent, and discerning if he holds his tongue" (Proverbs 17:28). She was so fascinated with the Scripture that she decided to experiment by practicing it at an upcoming party.

Normally Olivia loved to be in the center of socializing, but that evening she quietly observed. Instead of focusing on herself, she studied her friends and was surprised at how enjoyable they were to watch. Toward the end of the party, when many of the guests had gone, a young man walked over to Olivia and looked at her thoughtfully. Finally, he said, "You're very wise, aren't you?"

Olivia was astonished. Then she felt guilty. She didn't think she deserved his admiration. *I'm not wise; I was only quiet.* In reply to the young man, Olivia simply smiled. Later, as she thought it over, Olivia saw the value of holding her tongue and decided she had learned a wonderful secret from God's Word.

The poise of her quiet countenance attracted the young man. This also pleases God. "The unfading beauty of a gentle and quiet spirit . . . is of great worth in God's sight" (1 Peter 3:4).

Things That Scare Guys

Now that we've got the silly behavior thing figured out, let's look at a few other girl things that make guys break out in a sweat, rash or other allergic reaction. Yep. There's other stuff that can make guys want to run in the other direction. Not so much because it turns them off but more because it makes them squeamish. Guys just don't want to be a part of certain things that are in a girl's world. Let's call these things that scare guys.

Girls' Purses

Like girls' purses, for instance. No, a guy is not afraid you're gonna whop him with it. But . . .

> Whatever you do, don't ask a guy to do you a favor by retrieving something out of your purse.

Let's say, for example, you're in a restaurant with a group of friends, and your cell phone rings. It's in a pocket on the outside of your purse, so even though your fingers are sticky with barbecue sauce, you manage to answer it and prop it at your ear with your shoulder. Your mother's calling, with a quick message that needs writing down. One glance at your gooey fingers shows you there's no way you can rummage through your purse for paper and pen, so you do the logical thing. You turn to the person next to you, who happens to be a guy, and ask him to dig them out for you.

I know that seems like a simple enough request, but do you have any idea what goes through a guy's mind at that point?

Oh, no! What am I gonna do? A girl's purse is private, man. What if there are those female panty things or something in there? I don't wanna touch them; I don't even wanna see 'em!

The guy is trapped. You're looking at him, frantically motioning for pen and paper. But the guys at the table are looking at him too, with pity and also a certain measure of glee. They *know* what he's going through. What's their buddy gonna do? Whatever it is, it will definitely be good for a laugh later! And the guy knows it.

What's he going to do? The only thing a guy *can* do in that predicament. He grabs your purse as if it were a hot potato and hands it to a girl!

Her Room

When visiting in a home, a guy doesn't particularly like being invited to see a girl's room, for reasons similar to why he wants nothing to do with her purse. A girl's bedroom is *personal!* He doesn't want to take the risk of accidentally seeing something that he's not meant to see—panties, a bra that missed your laundry basket, even pajamas or a nightgown.

Undies in sight in your room may seem very insignificant to you. After all, it's just underwear, right? Yeah, but it's not just any underwear, it's *your* lingerie! Once a guy sees the color, the style, the lace . . . those items in *your* room, he must fight to keep from imagining them *on* you. He doesn't need his thoughts going in that direction.

Admittedly, guys have a curiosity about mysterious girl garments. They just don't want that fascination satisfied now.

> They know it will be when they're married, but until then, those secrets are off-limits.

(It's bad enough for guys walking past lingerie shops in the mall.)

Even married guys are uncomfortable in the lingerie section of a department store. Have you ever seen their expressions while their wives browse amid bras, camisoles and slips? Most of the guys pace in the aisle on the outskirts of the department. Those men would rather be *anywhere* than around all those feminine unmentionables.

There's usually an exception to the rule, and in this case it's Brady. A bunch of guys at our house told this story about him. When Brady saw one of the girls from his youth group in a lingerie store, he went in too. He walked over to where Christy was shopping, picked up a push-up bra and made a smart-alecky comment. Brady wasn't being suggestive; he was trying to be funny. But he happened to pick a feisty girl to tease and it backfired. Christy turned on him and said in tones not hushed, "Get out of here, you little creep!"

The guys got a good laugh over it, and so did I. Brady took the risk of invading a woman's domain and met his match. He got by with that prank because he and Christy were in a neutral zone. I seriously doubt he'd had the nerve to pull something like that if they had been in her home. (Any decent young man would know that he was clearly crossing the line there.)

This leads to another reason guys are reluctant to venture into a girl's room and that has to do with . . .

Meeting a Girl's Dad

Meeting a girl's parents is fairly stressful, period. But facing The Dad is a major hurdle for guys. Good dads are protective of their daughters. In order for a guy to win a girl's hand, he also must win the heart of her father. You know why that's so scary for a guy? Because dads are guys too—they know exactly how males think!

Can I encourage you to trust the discernment of your parents? When it comes to guys, your mom and dad have many more years of experience. You're precious to them; they want the very best for you.

[
A quality guy will never encourage you
to defy your parents.
]

Guys with genuine character are willing to face the scrutiny of a girl's parents. Keeping that in mind, not many good guys would dare darken the door of your bedroom without a parent beside them, or at least with their permission.

Girls Whispering

It doesn't matter what you're talking about. If you and other girls whisper together in front of a guy, he automatically assumes that you're probably talking about him. The fact that you're whispering instead of talking in a normal tone of voice tells him this, even if it's not true. If the guy is interested in one of the girls, that makes it all the more unnerving.

A guy isn't necessarily being egotistical because he feels self-conscious around your whispering. Haven't you felt that way when other girls were whispering around *you*? As a child you were no doubt taught that it's impolite to whisper in front of others. That's a good, basic rule for every occasion. Around a guy it can mean the difference between his seeing you as silly or mature.

Girls-Only Conversations

Guys feel the same about for-females-only topics. Guys *don't* want to hear you discussing the pros and cons of different styles of bras and panties. (Yes, girls do that. This list of things that scare guys is from the guys themselves.) I emphasize don't because the guys emphasize it. It gets their minds going where they don't want them to and it irritates guys when girls talk that way in front of them.

> They also find it embarrassing when girls talk among themselves about personal stuff around guys.

It is rarely, if ever, necessary to discuss your periods and other female matters in front of guys. They know that girls have periods . . . and cramps . . . and headaches . . . they know about PMS and that some females get moody once a month. But guys would rather not hear girls discuss it.

Even after they're married, you won't see a bunch of guys in an animated conversation discussing how long their wives were in labor, and what it was like seeing their babies born. Those details make them nauseous. Kind of amazing, isn't it, when you consider the gross stuff that guys *do* like to talk about. Oh, I never got specific, did I? OK, I'll tell you one story. Just keep in mind that this is being translated from guy talk. I can't bring myself to tell it quite the way they told each other.

Even though they had a long-distance relationship, there was no guessing how Heidi and Jason felt about each other. As often as possible, Heidi visited Jason's hometown. Those were short visits, so they both looked forward to spring break when Jason could make the hundreds-of-miles trek to see Heidi and stay for several days. Alas, those wonderful days passed quickly and before they knew it, the time came for them to part again.

Saying good-bye is never easy. A guy must tear himself away from his dream girl. Also, for a guy the actual parting is a moment that must be handled with delicacy because he wants his girl to feel assured and secure. That's a wonderful male inclination—desiring to protect her. From a female perspective, when a guy is leaving, we want inner peace—that settled feeling that everything is alright.

This all created quite a challenge for Jason. During that crucial and normally romantic moment with Heidi, Jason's stomach decided to complicate his parting. His intestines were seized with cramps and gas pains. And Jason was seized with panic. He needed to get to a bathroom. Now!

Meanwhile, Heidi gazed into his eyes with love and longing. *Don't go. Don't rush off. Just one more hug . . . why do you have such a pained expression on your face? Why do you seem so eager to leave?*

If ever there was a time Jason wanted to run, it was then. The truth be told, he *had* the runs.

So, are you laughing? The guys roared when they heard Jason's version. Poor Heidi. I hope she felt secure when he left.

Girls' Tears

[
When guys have a problem, they don't cry;
they try to solve it.
]

We girls try to solve our problems too, but we often do some crying in the process. It releases tension. When a girl sheds tears around a guy (and guys are natural fixers), he automatically assumes it's his responsibility to solve the problem. Sometimes he can't. (Most of the time, all we females want is for them to listen, anyway.) When there's nothing a guy can do, he feels helpless and inadequate. Panicky.

During my years as a single missionary, I often traveled in remote areas of northern Ontario where there were long wilderness stretches between communities. One bitter winter night, I made the decision to return to mission headquarters some two hundred and fifty miles away. I'm sure I had a reason the trip couldn't wait until morning, though I certainly can't remember it now. Lester, a young man who was engaged to be married, was going to the same town so he offered to drive the car.

It wasn't until we set out that we realized the car heater wasn't working properly. No matter, I thought, blankets were a normal part of survival gear when one traveled in the north. But frigid temperatures drop their lowest throughout the night, and pulling a blanket around me did very little to keep out the biting wind that rushed into every nook and cranny of the drafty old vehicle.

An hour can seem interminably long when you're chilled to the bone. *If I can just make it until we get to a gas station, we can warm up there,* I thought. But mile after mile went by. In the sparse villages that dotted the map, the couple stations we did see were closed.

Another hour went by. Even in my Sorels® boots with the felt liners, my toes stung painfully and began to grow numb. What about a house then? I was getting desperate to warm up, ready to request refuge anywhere. On that stretch of highway, in the black of night, a light in a window would show clearly. There were none. I'd driven the road dozens of times in the daytime and knew how desolate the area was. There would be no relief.

When I thought about how far we had yet to go, and knowing we could never make it on one tank of gas, the trip ceased to be an adventure. We were in genuine danger. This was one of those times when no guy could solve the problem. I reached the point where some tension needed to be released. I didn't sob but I shed some tears.

Lester panicked. "Don't cry!" he begged. "*Please*, don't cry!"

"I just need to cry a little bit," I tried to explain. I was so amazed at how flustered he was that I did stop crying. And started laughing.

"We need to pray!"

Now, the point of this story is to illustrate how guys get frustrated by girls' tears, but you probably want to know the outcome of this trip, so here goes . . .

We *did* pray! We prayed and we prayed. Mile after frigid mile we begged God to enable us to endure the cold, to multiply the gas until we could reach civilization. And he did. When we approached the outskirts of our destination, the neon lights of that open-24-hours-a-day service station were an enormously beautiful sight. I have no explanation for why we didn't run out of gas. I don't think you need one anyway, do you?

Guys are reluctant to be around girls' tears for another reason too . . .

Girls' Hearts

[
Giving your heart away to a guy when he's not
prepared to receive it can really scare him.
]

He may care for you a lot but still not want you to give him your heart. A guy doesn't want to be the keeper of it. He doesn't want to feel responsible for breaking it. He doesn't want to think he's the reason for your tears.

As much as Ethan wanted to build a relationship with Val, he chose to keep his distance. He made that decision because of his concern for her. Ethan knew his family would be moving away and he didn't want her heart to be broken. Nor his.

That poignant decision was a sign of an honorable guy.

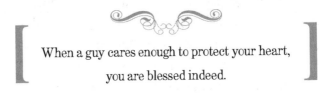

[
When a guy cares enough to protect your heart,
you are blessed indeed.
]

Your heart is too precious to give away lightly. "Above all else, guard your heart, for it is the wellspring of life" (Proverbs 4:23).

Marriage Makes a Difference

Much on this list changes after guys get married. To some extent then, they get over these things that scare guys. (Although they probably won't go to the grocery store to purchase certain items for you!) But until they say "I do," guys don't want to cross the line. (A single guy won't even consider changing a baby's diaper. But when he and his wife have their own baby . . . well . . . let's say it's at least more likely.) Most of these scary things, however, are still female issues and never become favorite topics for guys.

When married men get together, they sometimes compare notes and discover they're on common ground about the idiosyncrasies of their wives as females. And they laugh about it. But it's not malicious. They are celebrating our uniqueness. Men enjoy the mysterious ways of females—what they do, how they think—things that guys don't understand. Guys are all for those differences! But when it comes to females being silly, guys never outgrow their allergy to that.

Secret No. 7

Guys' Lives Don't Revolve Around Girls

Guys often joke about females being hard to understand, but it's rare for girls to laugh about the mysterious ways of guys. Maybe that's because most girls don't realize that guys *are* complex. When a girl takes a guy at face value only, she may unknowingly sabotage a potential friendship with him before it has time to develop. Or a girl may end up feeling hurt unnecessarily. Like Courtney . . .

I had a huge crush on Ricky; he was all I thought about. He seemed interested in me too. So when he said he'd call, I stayed home that Saturday and waited. I wasn't going to miss *his* call for anything! Amy and Alisha wanted me to meet them at the mall, but I told them I had to do something else. Well . . . I did! I had to stay home for Ricky's call! Not *everybody* has a cell phone, you know.

But the hours dragged by and the phone didn't ring. Finally, by midafternoon when I couldn't stand waiting any longer, I called him. Wouldn't you know . . . his *mother* answered!

"Ricky . . . it's for you."

"Who is it?"

"I don't know . . . but it's a girl."

I heard guys laughing . . . then footsteps getting louder. I wanted to hang up . . . too late . . .

"Hello?"

"Um . . . hi . . . this is Courtney. . . ."

"Hey, hi . . ."

Ricky was nice but he seemed eager to get off the phone. His friends were still joking around in the background. Obviously, he was having fun without me. I was devastated.

Though this young lady spent the day pining away for her guy, he didn't seem to be suffering while waiting to see her again. And Courtney did *not* understand.

It's easy to see why she felt hurt and confused, isn't it? There she was at home, dreaming about her crush, expecting him to call any minute. She put her life on hold and spent most of the day waiting for something that never happened. Only to finally discover—when *she* phoned *him*—that Ricky was having the time of his life with his friends! Oh, and yeah, he *was* going to call her—that evening.

I witnessed a similar scene when a girl phoned our home wishing to speak with one of our sons. The two were close friends, and I thought he'd be happy to receive her call. He wandered around the kitchen with the cordless, so I heard bits of his conversation. He was kind and polite, but he kept it short. In minutes he was back in his room where his buddies were hanging out.

So what's the deal? Were these guys interested in the girls or not? Before we look at answers to this question, let's take a little detour; it'll eventually take us right back to the question.

Besides the fact that both girls were left feeling puzzled and maybe hurt in the encounters they had with the guys, did you notice any other similarities? Okay . . . um . . . how about that both girls phoned the guys? We discussed this in an earlier chapter, and here are two more examples of the hazards girls can run into when calling guys.

When a girl phones a guy, chances are pretty good that he'll be occupied with something. When guys are busy, especially with their buddies, the odds of a girl's receiving a guy's full attention, either on the phone or while Instant Messaging, are significantly diminished. (In other words, he's not going to be fully tuned-in.)

Several guys were gathered in our home one evening when the phone rang. It was for Todd, a guest, and it was a girl. Guys were mingling all over and privacy was not an option, hardly the best circumstances for chatting with the girl.

Apparently, the young lady didn't pick up on this though. She must have had a lot on her mind because there were long pauses between Todd's short responses. After several minutes, he finally held the receiver away from his ear, looked at his buddies and mouthed the words, "She won't shut up!" The guys thought it was hilarious.

Todd wasn't being rude. He was embarrassed. That was not the right setting to have a meaningful conversation with this girl.

Instant Messaging a guy (or text messaging a cell phone) is at your own risk too. You have no way of knowing what's going on at the other end when your thoughts pop up on a guy's screen. If he's playing a game online, you're not likely to get his full attention. And he's not likely to tell you. I've seen a guy receive messages from two or three girls simultaneously while he's engaged in the drama of a furious online battle. Rather than savoring the conversations, he responded as rapidly as possible so as not to get blown away in the game. I think he rather enjoyed the added challenge, but the girls became an extension of the game, rather than his focus of attention.

Ladies, you're not too young to learn this insider tip for females:

> When you have something to say to a guy, it's good to know the best time to approach him. All moments are *not* equal!

Esther, in the Bible, understood this. When she had a burden on her heart to discuss with the king, she didn't just blurt it out. Esther carefully planned a time to talk with him when she would have his undivided attention. *And* when he would be in an amiable (good) mood (Esther 4-7)!

I wouldn't be at all surprised if you already understand this principle yourself. Hey, don't you pick and choose the best time to bring up important discussions with your mom or dad? Try applying your woman's intuition when it comes to communicating with guys!

How a guy feels about receiving a phone call from a girl can depend also on his relationship with her. If you have a *friend*ship established with a guy, some guys are fine about a girl phoning. But a guy may be less comfortable if a girl who is special to him initiates the first call. Not because he doesn't want to talk to her, but because he wants the call to take place in the right setting.

This brings us back to our question: *Were those guys interested in the girls or not?* After our little detour, I'm guessing you already know a portion of the answer. But there's more.

Guys' actions are easier to interpret, and this kind of hurt can be avoided, when you understand that guys' lives don't revolve around girls.

Wait a minute! Before you storm off in a huff, let me explain. From a guy's perspective, there are perfectly logical reasons for the way they act. Learning this secret can save you a ton of heartache, free you up for a lot more fun and spare you from getting into World War III with your favorite guy.

You mean guys don't think about girls 24/7? Well, yes and no. Guys think about girls—a lot! But even if a guy's interested in a girl, he'll still have a blast with his male friends. Girls are never far from guys' thoughts, but there are several good reasons they don't—they can't—let their lives revolve around girls. Let's put their rationale into four categories, each one starting with a *P*, so they're easier to remember.

Peter Pan Stage

In Secret No. 4, I said we'd take a closer look at the Peter Pan stage of guys. What was unique about the boys in the story of *Peter Pan?* They never wanted to grow up. Now it isn't that real boys don't want to grow up, but in several respects they do develop at a different rate than girls. Even though I read it all the time, I don't accept that boys are behind girls in their development.

> Males and females are different. When looked at
> as a group, boys are not lagging behind. In their
> maturation as guys, they are right on target.

Part of that development includes their Peter Pan stage. Guys like to goof off. It's a survival skill. Life can be pretty heavy for guys. Being able to unwind with fun and laughter helps them shake off the stresses that come with the responsibilities of leadership. In that respect, most males never do completely lose their little boy streak.

Have you ever heard women joke about counting their husbands as one of their kids? Maybe you've heard your mother say that about your dad. Wives who can laugh about this most likely have husbands who know how to de-stress. It's a whole different matter when a married man wants to hang out with the guys all the time and go play instead of taking care of his family. That's being irresponsible and immature.

But when guys your age spend most of their free time having a blast with their male friends, they're being normal guys. Notice, I said *free* time. That means when they're not carrying out their growing list of responsibilities, like studies, sports, church, civic and job commitments.

Guys can be in their upper teens—even college age and beyond (just ask your dad!)—and still wholeheartedly get into shooting potato guns, videotaping ridiculous stunts, playing paintball, racing remote control stuff and tinkering with Legos.® (In Minnesota, I saw an elaborate Lego® competition at the Mall of America. The contestants were serious engineering students from various colleges.)

One of the most common forms of guy fun has to do with creating explosions. I was first introduced to this phenomenon as I was growing up with my three sisters and four brothers.

During a few of those years, some of my brothers bunked in a room right next to the one I shared with my older sister. Those rooms were separated only by a makeshift "wall"—a drape suspended from a rod installed about five inches down from the top of the doorway. To get to the downstairs part of our house, my brothers had to knock on the molding before drawing aside the drape and passing through our room. It was frustrating to my brothers and more than a little scary for my sister and me. But we had no choice; we had to make the system work.

Now there's something important you need to know. For many years we eight siblings grew up without television. To this day I'm grateful because it forced us to invent our own entertainment. And my brothers became masters of that art.

Worrying about my brothers barging through our room while we were changing clothes was one thing, but I learned a new level of fear the day my brother decided to engage in a little creative guy fun in his room, instead of outdoors. I don't think I'd better name names, but here's what happened.

I was in my room minding my own girl business. On the other side of the curtain, however, unbeknownst to me, my brother was busily engrossed in breaking the heads off wooden stick matches and gingerly packing them, one by one, into his homemade rocket propulsion system, which also included gunpowder.

Suddenly, my peaceful concentration was ripped by a shocking *KA-BOOM!* What on earth? I looked up, and through the five-inch space between curtain rod and doorway, I watched a cloud of dark smoke mushroom upward and envelop the chandelier in my brother's room.

I jumped up from my bed, ran over to the curtain and, not bothering to knock, flung it to one side. My brother was lying facedown on his bed. Very still.

"Are you alright?" I cried, totally confused. "What happened? Are you OK?"

I waited. Finally . . . slowly . . . he turned over and sat up. His hair was singed in spots and his face was somewhat blackened. Still dazed, my brother perched on the edge of his bed for another moment, just staring back at me. Then he broke into a huge grin and started laughing hysterically.

That was by no means the only explosion my brothers exposed me to. But I don't remember any of the others occurring indoors. Undoubtedly my mother had something to do with that.

We females may never understand how blowing things up can be so exhilarating for guys, but I suspect males are born with an attraction for such entertainment. Or else it's hereditary. I've seen the same fascination in my own sons. There are times I could mean it very literally when I tell you my sons are having a "blast" with their male friends.

Preparation

It's normal for you to want a boyfriend. That's your "nesting instinct." But as we saw when we looked at their stages, high school and early-college-age guys' nesting instincts have not kicked in. They often have girlfriends, but they usually aren't as serious about the relationship as a girl may become. At that age, a guy knows he's not ready for a permanent commitment, whereas girls are thinking in terms of a mate.

Guys need time. To be ready for marriage, a young man must first concentrate on his education, developing a career and discovering his identity. Guys know how easy it is to get tripped up by temptations that come with a steady girlfriend.

> Those too-serious-too-soon relationships can actually distract and hinder a guy from the preparations necessary to become a quality husband and father. And what young lady doesn't prefer a quality guy?

Let's get practical. Say you're in love with a college guy who has a big semester final coming up. (This applies in high school too.) Rather than making him feel torn between studying and spending time with you, a wise girl will encourage her guy to take all the time he needs to become well prepared for that exam. Part of what it means to be a suitable helper is to assist and release a guy to do what is required for his success—with no guilt trips attached.

Keep in mind that there's a big difference between encouraging and nagging. Encouraging a guy by letting him know you have constructive things to do while he studies can be a relief to him. On the other hand, nagging a guy to study will not yield the same results. Encouragement motivates and builds up; nagging disheartens and tears down. Huge difference.

Instead of competing with your guy's classes, why not take some of that study time when he can't be with you to pray for him? The better he does in school (or in whatever career preparations he's making), the better equipped he will be when it's time for marriage. Long range, isn't that better for both of you?

At this point in your life, you're free to develop your own options as well. This isn't the time to put your life on pause while waiting for a husband. Even if you and a guy are committed to each other, remember that he is growing and developing as a person. Don't let your own life stagnate.

What if the greatest longing of your heart is to be a stay-at-home mom devoted solely to her family? This will still occupy only a portion of your life. Females tend to forget this when they daydream about living happily ever after with Prince Charming. The time comes when your children will be grown and on their own. Before marriage is an ideal time to explore, discover and cultivate your gifts and talents.

A "Proverbs 31 woman" has many roles and many seasons. The one you are in now is precious and extremely important. Use it wisely for yourself while cheering the guys on in their pursuits.

Performance

This point might ruffle your feathers a bit at first, but really, it's OK. Guys have a good reason for this one too.

> Guys don't depend on relationships with girls for their identity or fulfillment.

They find these in the things they do, such as sports, accomplishments, jobs and especially from their male friends. (We'll look closely at the friendship angle in Secret No. 8).

Since the Garden of Eden, men's main focus has been on the way they are able to take care of their families. Providing for and protecting families revolve around what guys *do*. Doesn't it make sense, then, that to a guy, what he does defines his identity?

When men meet for the first time, they normally ask each other, "What do you do?" The underlying question is, "Define your identity, your worth; how qualified are you to take care of yourself and your family?"

Among guys, the proving of oneself starts early. Baseball or football card collections are often a boy's first form of currency. The kid with the most collectable cards is the richest. If he happens to have valuable rookie cards, he's king of the neighborhood!

Competition among guys shows more and more as they grow up. And it gets very physical. By high school, lots of guys are seriously into sports. A guy's whole world may revolve around earning a place on the team. Competing for positions is fierce. Staying on the team involves discipline and commitment. And you *know* how intense *inter*school rivalry is!

But guys explore other forms of validating their self-worth too— academic achievements, jobs, excelling in specialized hobbies, mastering musical instruments—it varies according to what each guy sees as important. Or what he thinks *other* people expect of him.

> Eventually, each guy defines his own identity
> by what he does. When a guy is satisfied with
> his identity, he feels fulfilled. That's when a
> guy normally allows himself to *feel qualified*
> to have a girlfriend.

In his mind, having a girlfriend does not give him his identity; his identity (what he *does*) gives him confidence to have a girlfriend/wife. This should make it easy to understand why helping a guy do well is to *your* benefit.

I am not saying that a guy's performance is what gives him his identity. This is the normal way guys validate themselves. Similar to the way girls affirm their own worth according to how pretty they see themselves. Not really an accurate assessment, is it?

> Once a guy understands his position in Christ, he begins to learn that his identity is not merely in what he does but rather in *who* he is—God's creation.

After that, a guy can find *true* fulfillment when he lives out God's call on his life. (Your fulfillment comes the same way, not through how you look or who your steady is, but in your relationship with God and in fulfilling his destiny for your life.)

We females often complicate matters. When we oooh and aaah about guys' cars, scream over musicians in a band, fight each other over the popular guys and give our favors to the rich, we send a clear message to men about what we think of them—but also what we think of ourselves. It exposes our values. Guys have terms for girls who place too great an emphasis on the positions and material positions of guys: gold diggers, diamond miners and mercenaries. (I learned another term recently too—serial daters—girls who date around, show no loyalty and date more than one guy, even on the same day.)

Whether or not girls do it intentionally, guys intensely feel our pressure for them to perform. Since they already measure themselves by their achievements, it becomes an even greater burden. Guys feel forced to produce in order to be accepted by girls.

But . . .

[What guys really want from females is respect.]

That's no surprise when you realize it's backed up by Scripture! God *wants* us to show respect toward men (see Ephesians 5:33). Girls who make a guy feel valued for who he is, rather than for what he does or owns, can melt a guy's heart. A female who expresses her admiration to a guy for his *character* can make his head swim with wonderful thoughts. Girls like this make guys *want* to achieve great things!

Protection

Men are responsible to protect and provide for women and children. This is one of the main reasons guys can't let their lives revolve around girls. Duty comes first.

A clear example of this is the military. A guy in uniform may be deeply in love with his wife or fiancée. With all his heart he may yearn to hold her in his arms. But while he's on duty, he cannot break ranks to rush to her. He must stand at attention and stay at his post. During a formal ceremony, he can't even hold hands with his girl. When we look at the big picture, we see the absolute necessity for this kind of discipline in order for men to provide proper protection.

Men need to keep their priorities straight for the well-being of families but also to protect themselves. A man whose life revolves around a woman can become ineffective in his responsibilities and get himself in trouble!

Women's wiles have caused the downfall of many a man—in novels, movies and in real life. When a guy is first in love, it's easy for him to become vulnerable. That's when he desperately needs friends, family, God and duty to keep him tethered to reality.

Look what happened to Samson. His story is found in Judges 14-16. He cut his reality cord when he insisted on his own way instead of heeding the counsel of his parents. He ended up bound with real ropes. Samson lost his strength, his freedom, his eyesight and his ministry, all because he took his eyes off God's call on his life and allowed his life to revolve around Delilah instead. Yes, Delilah got her way. For a time, she had Samson's undivided attention. But in the end, she lost out too.

Aah, but there *is* a time when you *will* be the center of a guy's universe! That's during courtship. This is the time when a guy's life revolves around the girl of his dreams. Hmmm, notice something interesting here? Even when you're a guy's main attraction, it centers on what the guy is *doing*—he's pursuing you. What fun!

It really *is* fun, and I don't want to spoil things, but it's only fair to explain that this condition is temporary. If all a guy ever did was swoon over his mate for the rest of his life, he'd accomplish nothing. He'd be ill-equipped to take care of her or their children.

Does this mean we females are sentenced to take second place to a man's career? No way. What it means is that you can become very valuable to a guy! God brings a young lady into a guy's life so they will accomplish his purposes *together*. A woman is the inspiration that motivates a man.

Women may have different roles than men, but our goals need to be the same—God's will. With you at his side, he'll be more successful, more effective. You can be the main reason that your guy becomes a winner!

When a woman helps a man excel, she's helping him to live out his identity. And since that is where a man gets his fulfillment, a lady who enhances this in his life is going to be extremely precious to a man.

Quite honestly, I think that's why men sometimes fall for their secretaries or office coworkers. A guy goes to work and some young lady there helps him succeed in his job. That builds him up and he feels better about himself. This makes her precious to him. Perhaps he goes home to a nagging wife who treats him with disrespect and tears him down. Where do you think this man is going to want to be? Who do you think he will want to be with?

Is that a good excuse for a man to be unfaithful? No. But is it a reason? Yes!

Teamed up God's way, you'll see that you're by no means in second place to your man's job. A guy's career is not an end it itself; it's a means to an end—the glory of God and the welfare of his family. What a wonderful package when he can achieve this while doing something he loves!

But what about workaholics? Not all guys understand God's plan. Or else they reject it. Wives and families can and do suffer neglect when a guy is in love with his own identity, his job or money. Sometimes guys gradually glide into this lifestyle because of pressure from their wives to perform, produce and provide. A covetous wife can cause her husband's downfall and hurt herself.

Are you wondering what some of this husband-wife stuff has to do with you? After all, maybe you're still trying just to make it through high school. There's a reason I'm bringing out these points now.

[
If a guy's life revolves only around himself, there will be signs of this long before you marry him.
]

Here are a few things to watch for while you're getting to know guys:
- Does a guy ask questions about you or just talk about himself?
- Is he a good listener?
- Does he show an interest in other people?
- What is important to him?
- Is he compassionate?
- Does he pray?
- Does he know how to relax?
- How's his sense of humor?

With these tips, hopefully it'll be easier to sidestep guys who are hung up on themselves. Plus, if a guy is on the right track, there'll be plenty of indications.

Think about it. Do you really want to be the center of your guy's universe? Would you really want him swooning over you 24/7 instead of maturing and preparing for a future? When guys focus on matters other than girls, they aren't just protecting themselves; they're protecting you too. Help a guy keep his priorities straight and you both come out winners!

Should I Phone Him?

Here's an easy checklist for when you're thinking of phoning. (Keep in mind, though, it's only a reference to refresh your memory; it's not a list of laws!)

1. If you make the first call, you can't be confident of his degree of interest in you.

2. Pursuing a guy by phone can end a potential friendship before it begins.

3. When you phone a guy, chances are good that he'll be occupied. In that case, you won't get his full attention.

4. With other guys around, he'll likely cut the call short, even if he's interested in you.

5. If he's with friends, a guy is often embarrassed when a girl calls. That turns him off toward her.

6. Even if you're special to him, he may not want you phoning because he wants the right setting in which to chat.

7. _____

_____.

I didn't forget number seven . . . you'll find it in Secret No. 12! Keep reading.

Secret No. 8

❧

Guys Need Breathing Room

"There is almost nothing that ticks off guys more than a girl who takes a guy away from his friends!" Wow, those are some strong words, aren't they? This guy's intense reaction expresses the way many guys feel when their circle of camaraderie is broken by a possessive girl. Most girls have no idea how fervently guys feel about this, and certainly not *why* it's such a huge issue. Since it's that important to guys, it's worth us females taking a close look.

Diversion

During this time in their lives when hormones are surging, keeping busy with their friends is a powerful diversion for guys. In the last chapter, Courtney felt hurt when she phoned Ricky and discovered he was goofing around with his buddies while she stayed home doing nothing but pining away for him. It made perfect sense to Ricky though.

From his perspective, he was actively pursuing a healthy alternative to the temptations that guys experience when they have too much time to fantasize. Ricky may be crazy about Courtney, but at his age when marriage is obviously not in the immediate picture, what does he do with his longing for her?

Girls find a large measure of fulfillment in heart-to-heart talks with guys. After she hangs up from this kind of a conversation, a girl may float away in dreamy bliss, filled with the sheer joy of having just talked with her crush.

Guys appreciate soul intimacy too, but it doesn't have the same effect on them. Their greater form of fulfillment with a girl comes through physical intimacy. So after a guy hangs up the phone, his imagination is kicked into another gear. For his own well-being, instead of drifting away in romantic fantasizing, he needs to find a diversion to *halt* the daydreaming! It's a sensitive topic for guys. Their bodies scream, "Reproduce, reproduce!" But their circumstances command, "Not yet, not yet!"

Guys today hear yet another message from society. "Go ahead, go ahead." Tons of messages tell guys and girls alike that virtue and purity are passé, that everyone's doing it. But it's simply not true! As astonishing as it may seem, there are plenty of guys who, like you, want the self-respect of being honorable and chaste.

With the bombardment of sensory stimulation out there, guys must actively work at finding distractions. Spending time with their comrades is one of their constructive escapes. When a guy gathers with his buddies, devotes himself to a sport, stays busy with a job, keeps active in church, etc., he is making positive use of a time in his life that is fraught with temptations.

Since God created guys, he understands how they are wired. He is fully aware of the traps and pitfalls that males encounter, and because of this God is very protective of guys! He gave numerous (and I do mean numerous) Scriptures to guide them safely through those snares. Consider Proverbs 4:20, 23; 5:1-23; 6:20-29, 32-35; 7:1-27 for starters.

Isn't it interesting that these references are directed specifically toward guys? Why didn't God load the Bible with verses warning females about the pitfalls of sexual sins? Maybe it's because God's plan is orderly. When men obey God, they are an automatic covering for women. And when women obey God, they are gently and lovingly included in God's protection plan.

> If females lure guys into immorality,
> they destroy their own protection.

When we refuse the leadership of men, we're rejecting God's appointed guardians. Women who have been strongly influenced by the feminist movement may feel offended by this. But think about how God has entrusted men with our safety; think of how accountable this makes men to God! Guys need our prayers and support.

Definition

Hanging with the guys is also a time when males give and receive affirmation from each other as they are learning to be men. They're defining their roles and responsibilities. Guys want and need their own identities and a lot of this happens while they do stuff together.

It starts when they're small. A boy's first hero is his daddy. That little guy watches, listens and takes in everything Daddy does as his example of what it means to be a man. That's where he gets his first clues for a self-image. He trails his dad like a shadow and wants to be just like him.

As a boy gets older, he starts observing other men and his peers. We saw in their stages that boys gravitate toward other boys for survival and for practice in the art of being a guy. Their male-ness provides a common bond, and they become their own support group.

It's easy to understand why guys form street gangs. If they grow up in a tough environment, these guys band together to ensure their identity, strength and protection; they see it as necessary to their literal survival. And woe to anyone who weakens their gang!

> Regardless of their ages, all guys like to gather for events where it's a no-women situation. This has nothing to do with rejecting females.

But it has everything to do with men wanting and needing definition. They use these all-male get-togethers to affirm their identities and to strengthen and encourage each other.

There's an old saying, "Boys will be boys," but not every setting allows guys that space, particularly not when there are females around. Guys have learned that certain conduct is not cool in mixed company. (And aren't we females glad!) Hanging with the guys is that sacred time when they can drop their refinement and be uninhibitedly male. They also use their fellowship to apply peer pressure to get each other to shape up. They define and refine their roles as men, cheering on or razzing one another as they see fit.

Some things about being a male, or a female, can be appreciated only by the same sex because the experiences are common solely to that gender. For example, how might you and your friends react if you were discussing the challenges and details of monthly cramps and a guy invited himself into your circle and joined in with his opinions? I fear for that guy!

Would you react because you hate guys? Would it mean you never wanted them around? Of course not. It has nothing to do with rejecting men, does it? But the whole topic of women's monthlies is not within a guy's frame of reference. He can't relate, he can't help and he can't bond with girls by discussing it with them. In fact, he may actually alienate himself from them by invading that girls-only realm.

Guys need to be given the same respect for their privacy without girls protesting and crying "sexism." Don't take it personally when a guy chooses time with his friends. Guys love females, but there are times when they want and need to be with just other males.

[We need to learn when to give guys breathing room.]

Even though they may be polite to a girl who interrupts or joins in with the guys, it doesn't necessarily mean she's welcome. Not even if she's a girlfriend to one of them. Believe me; females lose nothing by giving guys their space. If anything, it's the other way around. Once guys have built each other up, they're even more eager to mix with girls again!

Defense

In the old cowboy movies, a wagon train would form a circle at night as a strategy for defense. By sticking close together, they kept track of each other and kept threats at bay. The camaraderie of guys is like that wagon train. It's their circle of defense. Guys draw strength and security from their accountability to each other.

When guys see one of their cohorts pulled away from them by a girl who demands all of his attention, guys resent it. They feel that weakens their group. They feel it diminishes the safeguards for each individual guy. And they see it as a threat to their friend's welfare. They feel he's being snared into a relationship that they know can't be healthy at their age. Besides, guys are always wary of possessive females. Guys figure that if a girl's motives are pure, there's no need for her to isolate a guy.

Cody met April at the clothing store in the mall where they worked. They were often assigned the same shift. He liked April's outgoing personality and was impressed with her retail sales record. During their breaks, April coaxed Cody to go with her for cappuccinos at the food court. Cody felt a little guilty because they returned to their shifts late, more often than not. But that's where their relationship started to grow, and he enjoyed her company. She was upbeat and energetic.

One day, April showed up in the junior college student lounge where Cody studied with his friends. He was completely surprised, taken off guard.

"C'mon, Cody. Let's go for lunch."

"Uh, OK, sure." Scooping up his books, he looked at the guys, shrugged and gave them a wan smile. They looked at each other and shrugged too. *So much for Cody's trig test.*

In the days and weeks that followed, Cody's buddies saw him less and less. On the rare occasions when they did see him, he was with "that girl."

April often phoned Cody. Each time his parents asked him to bring her home to meet them, she had an excuse for not going. Cody's family saw less and less of him too.

Over time, his grades dropped. That put him on probation with the basketball team, and he was their star center! When he finally was kicked off the team for missing practices and showing up late for games, April broke up with him.

Cody's world had completely crumbled. Where did he go from there? His buddies were disgusted, his family was hurt, his grade point average tanked, his teammates were angry and now that his prestige was gone, so was his girlfriend.

When a guy disses his friends for a girl, it can be difficult for him to be accepted in his circle of friends again. They see him as a sellout. In his favor, though, is the mercy which guys eventually extend to a brother who, in their eyes, has been the victim of a controlling girl.

As for the girl, the guys red-flag her; they'll remember her and keep their distance.

For any young lady who wants to keep a guy to herself, there's one more consequence that could be the greatest deterrent of all.

> Once a girl succeeds in cutting her guy off from other influences in his life, she might discover that she has destroyed the qualities in him that attracted her in the first place.

In essence, she ruined what she wanted to own.

Hey, you're right. Guys can be possessive too. Let's park on this thought for a minute. Any guy who tries to pull you away from *your* friends or come between you and your parents is bad news! He can even be dangerous. Here are a few red flags to watch for.

Does He . . .

- have a history of bad relationships or past violence?
- always blame his problems on other people?
- blame you for "making" him treat you badly?
- try to control you by being bossy?
- minimize your emotions (not take your opinions seriously)?
- make fun of you, put you down or embarrass you in front of other people?
- try to violate your physical boundaries?
- decide who you see, what you wear, what you do, etc.?
- isolate you from family and friends?

Do You . . .

- feel less confident about yourself when you're with him?
- feel scared or worried about doing or saying "the wrong thing"?
- find yourself changing your behavior out of fear or to avoid a fight?

These guys do not have your best interests in mind. Stay away from them. No matter how much you long to have your own boyfriend, or how flattering a guy's attention may seem, don't sacrifice your peace for a guy. Remember, God has promised to supply *all* your needs (Philippians 4:19). Ask your heavenly Father to supply the love, attention and emotional security you need. God's ways are safe, healthy and fulfilling.

(Note: These red flag points are from the National Domestic Violence Hotline, 1-800-799-SAFE [7233]. They apply to abusive girls as well! For more helpful information, check out www.ndvh.org/teens.html.)

Free or Flee

Guys don't like feeling manipulated, controlled or emotionally cornered by a girl. Being conquerors, they naturally withdraw from those situations. For many guys, the more they feel pressured by girls to make commitments, the more they pull away. They wish guy-girl stuff was more relaxed and that there was less pressure to pair off. During an all-guys discussion, one lamented . . .

["Why do girls get leechy when you're nice to them?"]

He wanted the friendship but without the pressure. In a survey, more than one guy wrote, "Let us go after God."

I've heard similar statements with my own ears. Sometimes guys feel hounded by girls and express irritation over it. One guy grew so tired of being chased that he finally confronted the girl. Thankfully, he was diplomatic. He was one of those rare guys who did reveal a few secrets to a girl. He gave the young lady tips on relating to guys without ticking them off, and he still managed to be her friend after that (but not her boyfriend)!

Countless girls have ended up feeling hurt after they insisted on cornering a guy into a relationship. Remember, guys don't like guy vs. girl situations, so a guy may reluctantly consent to a declared relationship for a time, fully intending to eventually cut it off.

A girl can invest years in a certain guy, only to discover that she isn't really his choice. Guys may allow persistent girls to get them involved in a relationship, but this doesn't mean the girl is going to benefit by it. The sad part of this is, when they finally break it off, the girl is left feeling dumbfounded, wondering what the whole thing was all about. If she thought back, she might see that she had been the aggressor. Hey, it feeds guys' egos to have girls pursue them. (We've already talked about this plenty but it bears repeating: the girl who's *not* pursuing is the one who catches a guy's interest!)

Jealousy Unveiled

Controlling females scare the matrimonial daylights out of guys! When it comes to a permanent relationship, this is one topic about which guys *do* daydream! But probably not the way you'd expect. I've heard their hilarious bull sessions. They fantasize about what it could be like marrying a certain girl only to have her turn into "Wife-zilla the control freak!" They picture the nightmare of constant nagging. They laugh over Scriptures like "a quarrelsome wife is like a constant dripping" (Proverbs 19:13) and "Better to live on a corner of the roof than share a house with a quarrelsome wife" (Proverbs 21:9). That verse is in Proverbs twice! (See also Proverbs 25:24.) Could God be trying to tell us something? These verses were penned by Solomon, who had 700 wives and 300 mistresses (1 Kings 11:3). I think he knew a little something about living with women!

[
If a girl shows signs of possessiveness,
guys would rather end a relationship than
take the risk of living the rest of their lives in a
marriage where the woman rules the roost.
]

They shudder at the thought of endless years of "yes, dear," with no way out.

Sean was sure he'd found a prize catch when he met Marcy. He thought she was feminine, quiet, talented and fun to be with. On top of that, he *really* liked the way she looked; Marcy was one special girl.

As the months went by, Sean carefully worked on building a friendship with her. All seemed to go perfectly; he felt they were getting along great. Marcy was never far from his thoughts. Even though they had made no formal commitment, he had no desire to look at other girls. Until one day when something happened which grated on Sean like a skipping CD player.

He and Marcy both had busy schedules and hadn't seen each other for a few days. Naturally, Sean wanted to reconnect, so he phoned her.

"Hi, Marcy."

"Oh . . . hi."

"I miss you."

"Oh, *really?*"

Sean had never heard that tone of voice from Marcy before. "Yeah. School has been a bear . . ."

"That's not what *I* hear."

"What? What do you mean? . . ."

"Oh, never mind. I gotta go."

"Marcy! What's going on?"

"Like you don't know . . . what about Lily Mason?"

"Yeah, we studied together before our Spanish quiz on Thursday. She's fun . . . but what about her?"

Silence.

"Marcy?"

"What?!"

Marcy was clearly upset but Sean was clueless. "You sound busy, Marcy. I'll catch ya later."

Marcy let out a heavy sigh. "Well, are you coming over tomorrow night, or not?"

"I'll have to let you know . . . see ya."

Sean hung up stunned. That was *not* the Marcy he knew! But it *was* Marcy . . . and he felt annoyed. Where did she get off talking to him like that? If this was all because he and Lily helped each other before that quiz, Marcy had a problem! Where did she hear about that anyway? Not that he'd been sneaking around . . . what's there to hide when you're crazy about your girl? Marcy was the joy of his heart . . . but if she was gonna act jealous just because he talked with another girl . . .

Sean wasn't sure if he felt more hurt or more relieved. *If that's the kind of girl she is, I'm thankful I found out now!* In Sean's mind, that sarcastic and jealous side of Marcy had turned her into "Wife-zilla," every guy's nightmare. As much as he regretted their relationship fizzling, Sean was determined that he would not be owned by a female.

Did you happen to notice what Sean said about Lily? He had no personal interest in her, but he described her as fun. Another word for *fun* might be *enjoyable*. Guys want to *enjoy* being with a girl. A girl's attitude can make a world of difference.

Even though Sean and Marcy weren't officially going steady, the fact that they were close friends and spent a lot of time together did communicate a measure of devotion to one another. So we can see why Marcy may have felt a little jealous over Sean and Lily's studying together. But it was Marcy's attitude that spoiled things. Let's revisit their conversation and see how she could have communicated her apprehension in a healthier way.

"Hi, Marcy."

"Oh hi, Sean!"

"I miss you."

"I miss you too. How was your Spanish test yesterday?"

"It went better than I thought it was gonna, thanks to Lily Mason. We drilled each other on vocab right before class."

"Yeah, I heard. Wish it could have been me helping you."

"Me too. Lily's fun, but . . . "

"But what?"

"She's no substitute for you."

"Really? You know what, Sean? I have a little confession to make. I was feeling kind of jealous of Lily."

"Believe me, you have nothing to feel jealous about. Hey, I can hardly wait to see you tomorrow."

By the time Sean hung up from *this* conversation, he would have been on Cloud Nine! Marcy cared about him! And Marcy? Well, how would this conversation have made *you* feel?

Suppose when Marcy admitted she felt jealous, Sean had said, "Get over it, Marcy!" That would have revealed a side of Sean that *Marcy* needed to see! A positive attitude and communication are the keys. It's a good idea to practice these skills now, before you're married.

Benefits of Breathing Room

Hanging tightly to a guy is not going to make your relationship with him more secure. As we've seen, it usually does just the opposite. It can destroy a relationship that otherwise had a lot of promise.

> A girl with a special interest in a guy would be wise to not occupy or demand all of his time.

The benefits of giving guys breathing room are numerous and worth far more than the momentary "security" of having a guy under your control.

• Offering a guy breathing room gives him the space he needs to develop a strong, healthy personality.

• Making way for breathing room allows a guy to prepare for a promising future.

• Being nonpossessive is another of those traits that males like! When a girl is relaxed and enjoying life, it makes her all the more attractive.

• When a guy is not corralled, it frees him to think clearly and opens the way for the chase!

• Set guys free by being at peace with yourself. When you're not dependent on guys for your fulfillment, you're actually succeeding in maintaining some of that mystery that's so alluring to males! Girls who are their own persons, without being rebellious or haughty, challenge guys. Self-assured friendship and kindness work like a magnet.

• Not being possessive is good practice for issues that will crop up later. (Hint: It has to do with other key people in your life. We'll cover that issue but not here.)

Once guys are ready for marriage, some reasons for the camaraderie they need now will change. By the time they reach the altar, guys will gladly go their different directions with their wives. But even after they're married, guys are still going to need freedom to breathe. Nobody wants to feel imprisoned in a marriage. A guy who's happily married isn't going to feel a need to escape. Guys return to a source of pleasure! But guys will still need their time with other men, just as you will want time to socialize with other women.

When you understand why guys need their space, it makes sense to give it to them, doesn't it? That's not always easy to do when you're head-over-heels about a guy. But if you settle this in your heart now, it can save you a ton of heartache. It also gives your relationship room to grow. And after all, doesn't any growing thing need room to breathe?

Secret No. 9

Guys Are Vulnerable

Please raise your right hand and repeat after me: "I promise that I will never use the secrets revealed in this chapter to take advantage of guys or to use as a weapon against them."

OK, I'm not *really* asking you to make an oath, but we're about to take a behind-the-scenes look at a part of guys that girls rarely see. This is sacred information. In some ways, it might seem wiser to keep *these* secrets secret. But I think you deserve a closer look at the sensitive side of guys. Once you see it, your compassion and power of influence have the potential to make an astonishing impact in this world and in God's kingdom!

A Common Myth

When it comes to emotions, guys are often put into no-win situations again. It's a common myth that guys are hard-hearted. They're seen as cold and heartless, with no feelings. Or when they do openly show deep emotion, they're seen as weak and wimpy. Both of these views are extreme and inaccurate.

The truth is that men (and women) are made after God's image (Genesis 1:27). Since that's the case, and God expresses all kinds of emotions, it should be a reasonable assumption that guys would express all kinds of emotions too. But there are a couple of problems. First, our culture doesn't make allowances for guys to express many emotions. (Well, there are a couple of exceptions—they're expected to exhibit anger and lust. Pretty pitiful, isn't it?) And second, we fail to recognize the *ways* guys manifest their feelings.

Guys experience the same basic sentiments as the rest of the human race, (meaning females). They can feel vulnerable, defensive, rejected, fearful, anxious, embarrassed, humiliated, hurt . . . the list is endless.

The misunderstanding about how and what guys feel—or whether they feel *anything*—occurs because there's such a big difference in the way guys respond to their feelings compared to the ways girls handle their heart issues. Neither way is right or wrong—just different. (*Wrong* is gender-neutral. It comes on the scene only when guys and girls make unhealthy choices based on their emotions.)

Strong and Silent

Though most guys don't think in romantic daydreams, they're capable of caring deeply. And here's what's so heartrending. Sensitive emotions can be even *more painful* for guys than girls to deal with because society doesn't give guys the freedom to vent intense feelings. As a result . . .

[Guys don't express themselves as easily or readily.]

Emotions are still there but guys keep them inside. They tend to suffer in silence . . . and alone.

For example, when a young man is hurt or upset, instead of confiding in a buddy, he's more likely to do something physical.

Damien and Hailey have been going together for almost a year. However, at this very moment, they've just ended a phone conversation after breaking up. Let's look in on them.

Hailey

Sitting cross-legged on her bed, Hailey snapped shut her cell phone and listlessly tossed it toward her pillow. She stared at it for a moment. Breaking up was the right thing to do. She knew it. They both had agreed they were getting too involved physically.

Hailey glanced from the phone to the framed photo on the nightstand. It showed her and Damien biting the same piece of pizza. Even though their pupils looked red in that shot, it was still her favorite picture of them. *That was such a fun time.* Tears sprang to her eyes. She reached out blindly, grabbed the frame and placed it facedown, then buried her face in her pillow. *This is just too painful.* The bed shook with her sobs.

When she finally caught her breath, she fumbled for her phone, found Franny's name and pushed speed dial.

"Franny, . . ." Hailey's voice, so familiar to her best friend, changed to a wail, "we just broke up!"

"Hailey! How could you? What happened?"

"Well, you know how I've been telling you that Damien and I . . ."

You already know what Hailey is going to confide to Franny so let's see how Damien's handling it.

Damien

Damien reached out and set the cordless back on the recharger. He flopped back on his pillow with his hands behind his head and stared at the ceiling. *Now what?* His stomach churned.

Damien turned his head and spotted their pizza shop picture on his bulletin board. *Hailey's hair is so shiny.* He jumped up and made a bee-line for the photo, pulled out the pushpin and threw the picture in his bottom dresser drawer where it rested amid CD liners, a hodgepodge of forgotten baseball cards, unmatched shoelaces and other stuff he never looked at. Damien's stomach churned again.

He fled his bedroom and took the stairs two at a time down to the landing. Then he bolted through the dining room and out the back door, headed straight for the basketball hoop on Sherm's garage, two houses down.

Shot after shot, Damien dribbled and threw. Dodging, twisting, running, jumping, until finally, exhausted, he headed back home.

For two weeks, Damien spent his spare time shooting hoops at the neighbor's. But he never said a word about Hailey to anyone. And though his buddies heard the breakup rumor through the grapevine, they knew better than to bring it up; if he wanted to talk about it, he would.

> Guys communicate with each other even by
> what they don't say. And guys understand.

But to an outsider, Damien looked like he could not have cared less.

Offering His Heart

When a guy gives his heart to a girl, he's making himself extremely vulnerable. He is opening himself up to one of the most—if not *the* most—agonizing emotions on earth: rejection.

Girls have an outlet for the pain when they experience rejection. They can cry and talk with other people about how they feel. The hurt is very real indeed; but they have ways to work through it, and there's no shame attached to revealing their misery.

For guys, however, experiencing rejection is a more complicated maze to find their way through. Most guys don't react the way girls do. To do so would invite even more rejection from a wider scope of people. So guys are stuck dealing with their anguish by themselves. The isolation can intensify the pain and make it take longer to heal.

As a result, guys are generally more careful and much more reluctant to make serious commitments in a relationship. A girl might make a guy's head spin . . . but is she safe? A guy wants and needs a girl whom he can trust with his heart.

God delights in trustworthiness and says it makes a woman more valuable than jewels! "Who can find a virtuous woman? For her price is far above rubies. The heart of her husband doth safely trust in her" (Proverbs 31:10, 11, KJV). "A wife of noble character is her husband's crown" (Proverbs 12:4).

[

The young lady who won't play games
with a guy's heart is a gem.

]

Seeing how vulnerable guys are, can you imagine what they must go through in approaching a girl for the very first time? Or in asking her out? We females laugh about this—we know how approachable we are, right?

Wait a second! Many girls are now more than approachable! There's a growing trend on the horizon. Have you seen it? Maybe you're part of it. Females are starting to express their independence by being the aggressors. "Why should men be the ones who get to choose?" girls complain. It's their rationalization for asking guys out on dates. Modern young women see themselves as victims of the whims of guys who get to choose their pick of females!

That is so funny! If they heard guys talk among themselves, girls would laugh at how comical their victim mentality is. Guys see it exactly the opposite! They feel as if *they* are at the mercy of women! Any girl can reject an interested guy, so guys feel this puts them at the disadvantage! It might take a guy weeks, or even months, to get up the nerve to ask you for a date, and in a heartbeat you can turn him down cold.

Granted, his invitation could be a last-minute thought. Based on how well you know a guy, you might have clues about that. But maybe not. Since guys hide feelings, he may have been "testing the waters" for much longer than you realize before revealing his interest.

Every time a guy makes overtures toward you, he is temporarily giving you the power to wound him. Highlight that last sentence with a marker. It's so important I'm even going to repeat it! *Every time a guy makes overtures toward you, he is temporarily giving you the power to wound him!* Doesn't it melt your heart to know the price guys will pay for your attention?

A guy's view of himself together with his level of interest in a particular girl determine the degree of his vulnerability. This means that any time a guy approaches a girl, there can be a variety of factors at play. If he's a fairly confident guy and he enjoys you but isn't interested in getting serious, he may still want to ask you out. In those circumstances, your response may not be that big of a deal to him. Then again, a guy who isn't quite as confident, and who has a total crush on you, may feel that the very beating of his heart hinges on your reaction!

[
Even a self-assured guy can lose his nerve
when he's discovered the girl of his dreams.
]

Remember Dustin and Sage (in Secret No. 3)?

My sources told about one young man who grew tired of feeling intimidated about girls. One day in the mall he saw a young lady and was instantly smitten. Throwing caution aside, he boldly approached her and said—and, mind you, this was in front of her mother!—"You are, by far, one of the most beautiful girls I have ever seen in my life!"

According to the report, the girl blushed several rosy shades, then finally blurted, "Thank you."

And, totally bowled over by the young man's charm, her mother gushed, "Oh, that's so sweet!"

As far as romance goes, nothing came of that chance encounter. But it did a ton to strengthen the guy's ego and free him from the paralyzing fear of approaching girls. I'm certain it did nothing to spoil that girl's day either, though perhaps she's wishing she'd run into that guy again!

What must it be like for a guy to propose marriage? At that stage, a guy's defenses are all down! This is poignantly portrayed in the tradition of a man getting down on one knee in front of his lady love. It's an act of true humility and vulnerability—not easy for a guy! Hopefully by then he will know his girlfriend so well that his chances of being turned down are slim. And, hopefully, any young lady won't let a relationship reach the proposal stage if it's going nowhere.

Does a guy's vulnerability mean a girl is obligated to receive his attention? No, but if you're not interested in a guy, try to remain kind while letting him know. He may *appear* bold in his approach, but inwardly the guy may be quaking.

And let him know early. Some girls will go out with a guy for a while just to avoid hurting him. That's not a good idea. He views your dating him as a sign of a growing relationship. In the long run, this can hurt him more.

> There are ways to avoid devastating guys with rejection. In fact, it's possible to steer your friendship with a guy without using rejection at all!

Here are a few pointers:

• Don't play games with guys' emotions. Don't try to make him jealous. It may feel good to have a guy's affection, but it's not fair to juggle with his heart. A guy's heart becomes fragile the moment he entrusts it to a girl.

• Don't feed your ego by implying interest in a guy if it's not genuine. Teasing and fake attention get on guys' nerves. Behind-the-scenes conversations among guys reveal it's a major strike against girls. In all honesty, teasing is an explosive issue. It provokes anger in a guy. It's also selfish.

• Try to communicate clearly so a guy understands the nature of your friendship with him. If you think he's becoming romantically interested but you see him only as a friend, gently let him know where you're coming from by casually talking about other guys in your conversations. Bring up other girls as well. This helps him see that you don't view yourself as special to him.

• Another way to distance yourself from an unwanted suitor is to spend less time with him. Having heart-to-heart talks with a guy on a regular basis makes a statement to him. If you see your friendship growing in a direction you don't intend, cut back on those soul talks. Quit sharing your heart.

Ideally, a godly relationship *should* begin with a connection of the spirit and soul. (Instant physical attraction is not the best gauge for whether or not a guy could be a future love interest.) If you find yourself bonding with a guy through heart-to-heart discussions, you might want to pay attention. Perhaps you're developing a healthy relationship! Would you spend time sharing your thoughts with a guy if the two of you weren't connecting in your souls? Maybe you don't want to distance yourself from him after all. But above all, be careful not to lead him on.

• Guys don't want girls' pity. A guy is paying tribute to you when he reveals his interest. Be compassionate, but don't feel sorry for him if you're not interested in return. One of the nicest things you can do for him is to give him respect. This enables him to walk away with his heart intact.

Guys and girls need to be very careful about getting into a committed relationship when they're too young to follow-up on that devotion.

[
Repeatedly having your heart broken
can scar and harden it.
]

It can make each following relationship seem less valuable than the previous one. Can you see how going with and breaking up with several boyfriends is practice for divorce?

Pain Is Temporary

When Damien and Hailey broke up, it wasn't an issue of rejection; it was a mutual decision. Still, after being so close for so long, the pain of going separate ways was excruciating.

Let's take a moment to talk about heartbreak. It's too real and too common to ignore. It's a mistake to underestimate the depth of hurt guys and girls can feel over relationships. Romeo and Juliet aren't the only young people who thought of taking their lives because of lost love.

But suicide is never a good idea. Things change. No matter what you face, no matter how unbearable or hopeless your circumstances may seem today, they are only temporary. Therefore, we must find temporary solutions. And suicide is *not temporary.* Taking your physical life does *not* provide a final escape from emotional pain. Do you realize that you don't have it within your power to end your own existence? Not even by taking your physical life! God created man as an eternal being, so your life will go on.

Our heavenly Father understands how painful life can feel and how hopeless it may look. The Bible says that Jesus suffered all the same temptations that man faces (Hebrews 4:15). Could Jesus have been tempted with thoughts of suicide? That's a shocking thought, isn't it? But it's also comforting. Jesus understands! He does not condemn those who have failed or those who are hurting. "God did not send his Son into the world to condemn the world, but to save the world through him" (John 3:17).

God not only offers solutions for every temporary problem, but also offers the hope of an eternity full of joy for all who will trust him! Nothing is impossible with God (Luke 1:37). Through Jesus there is always hope. Always!

There was a time when my life was so painful that it seemed unbearable. I considered suicide, but I thought about how that would end any opportunity for things to get better. So I prayed instead. When I look back on that now, I'm so glad I prayed. Incredibly wonderful things have happened in my life since that awful time! I would have missed out on so much if I had given up. (And I would have hurt so many people and broken God's commands.)

Maybe *you* have a broken heart. Can I pray with you right now?

Dear heavenly Father,

Thank you that even when I feel like giving up, you don't give up on me. It's a relief to know that you understand when I'm hurting. Everything seems bleak and hopeless, and it's difficult to see the truth when I feel like this. But your Word says that your compassions are new every morning and your thoughts toward me are good. You have hope and plans for my future. And you've promised to send the Holy Spirit as my comforter. Please help me, Father. Thank you for caring. Thank you for loving me. I will wait for you to show me the way.

In Jesus' mighty name I pray, Amen.

If you prayed this prayer, please take one more step and talk with someone you trust, like your parents, your youth pastor, a teacher or youth leader. Whatever it is that hurts you now is temporary. God has wonderful plans for your future.

Other Reasons for Vulnerability

Guys are vulnerable and grieve for reasons other than girl trouble. Their emotions come out at times too, in a variety of ways, and often when they're alone. If you're alert to the symptoms, sometimes it's noticeable. Most of the time in public however, guys appear as macho as always.

• In his own room, Bob cried for days when his best friend moved away.

• Jacob lost weight and his grades dropped when his parents got divorced.

• Many nights Pete cried himself to sleep because he wasn't growing as fast as other guys.

• When Joe's sister was hospitalized as a result of a skating accident, he channeled his worry into shoveling snow. He cleared the whole block!

• Zach was devastated by his acne. It was too embarrassing to talk about. His misery was multiplied by dealing with it alone.

• Steve was a football all-star. The entire community claimed him as their hero. But his home life was miserable, and he confided that he deliberately chose to deal with his pain and anger on the field through that rough contact sport. "I wanted to smash some bodies," he said.

Guys tend to be naturally rough-and-tumble people; they love sports. So this does not mean that every time a guy is involved in a sport, he's hurting. But . . .

> Physical activity is a prominent method that guys use to let off steam and get rid of pent-up emotions.

It's their "body language." And since it's such a common way for guys to deal with their pain, I can't help but wonder what this says about the upsurge in extreme sports in the past twenty to thirty years. Is it just a coincidence that these life-threatening sports are gaining prominence with guys, parallel to the militant feminist movement? Or are they another sign that we have a culture of hurting males?

Vulnerable, But Not Weak

We've looked at a few things that bother guys and some of the ways they respond to their feelings. Whether or not a guy openly reveals how he feels is not an indicator of his strength. Guys who show their emotions aren't less male because they're expressive. Guys who keep their feelings inside aren't manlier; neither are they weaker because they don't pour out what they feel. Guys are people. They have vulnerable spots just as girls do. Being vulnerable is not a sign of weakness. It verifies that God created men and women to complement each other. He intended the genders to need each other (see 1 Corinthians 11:11, 12).

So what does it mean to us ladies when we see guys' vulnerability?

Girl Power

Have you ever imagined what it would be like to have superpowers like the female cartoon characters on TV or in the movies? Wouldn't it be great to have superhuman strength, speed, sight, intelligence . . . ? Nearly everyone at one time or another dreams about being able to fly. Even the rising interest in the occult and witchcraft is evidence that there's a craving for power. But most likely, as you fantasize about having super powers, you tell yourself, "If I could fly, had megastrength, etc., I'd use it for good."

Well, I have incredible news. You *do* have power . . . and in no small measure! You have it within your grasp to literally change the world! What's even more exciting, this power has been given to you by God.

That's right.

> God has entrusted to females
> the power of influence.

It all started back in the Garden of Eden when the Lord formed Eve and presented her to Adam as a "helper suitable for him" (Genesis 2:18).

Can you imagine what it must have been like for Adam as he looked at all the animals while he was naming them? How could he help but notice that each creature had its own mate but that he had none? Then, one day, Adam wakes up and . . . look what God has brought to him! A woman! Va-va-va-voom! Eve was flawless, perfect in every way, definitely "a ten" in guy terms.

Adam must have been ecstatic. The Bible doesn't say what Adam thought, but we do know that Eve had a tremendous amount of influence in Adam's life. When she offered him the forbidden fruit, even though he clearly knew what God had said about it, he chose to do what Eve did. He ate it too. "The rest," as they say, "is history."

"It's All Eve's Fault"

Have you ever forgiven Eve? It's pretty commonly accepted that she is the one who got us females into trouble, isn't it? Haven't we been under a curse all this time because she sinned in the garden? Wasn't it her bad influence on Adam that got the rest of us girls into this mess?

Hmmm. I've got some really good news, but before we talk about it, we'd better let Eve off the hook. It's time to forgive her. The first reason is obvious. We can't hold a grudge against anyone if we want to receive forgiveness ourselves (Matthew 6:14, 15). Second, probably every female who has ever lived has been a bad influence on a male at one time or another. Go ahead, take stock. Have you been absolutely perfect in your attitude and actions toward your dad, brothers, guy friends, classmates? Always?

Me neither. One time when I was in seventh grade, I had a terrible crush on a guy I'll call Nick. He had a crush on me too. We talked on the phone and spent time together at group events. I can't explain why I did certain things when I was that age but that was pretty young to have a boyfriend; it was exciting but also a little scary.

One day, there was a knock on our back door. When I opened it, there was Nick! I was *not* expecting him! I felt so flustered that I shut the door in his face and wouldn't open it again. Poor Nick. He was left standing there. You can imagine how much hurt and rejection he must have felt.

Now that I understand how vulnerable guys are, I'm even sorrier for that day. As a mother, when I think of a girl doing that to one of *my* sons . . . well . . . grrrr! It's embarrassing to admit to something I'm telling you *not* to do. But that's exactly why I'm revealing these roadblocks in relating with guys. If only someone had told me these secrets!

Ladies, our power of influence is much greater than you might at first realize. Guys are well aware of it. Think about advertising and you'll quickly get the picture. Everything from cars to snack chips is sold by using a girl in the ad, right? Guys are powerfully influenced by our sexuality! The whole issue of immodesty is wrapped up in . . . er . . . is unwrapped . . . oh, you know what I mean—uncovering our bodies is a misuse of our influence.

"Eve" Redeemed

Eve was supposed to be a suitable helper for Adam;
but by enticing him to disobey God,
she used her influence the wrong way.

Now that we recognize our own guilt for the same sin, what's the next step? It's not so much a step as it is a realization. Here's where the good news comes in.

Before Jesus was crucified, his disciple Peter denied him three times. After Jesus rose from the dead, he gave Peter the opportunity to reaffirm his love when he asked three times if Peter loved him. After Peter's earnest response, Jesus told him, "Follow me!" (John 18:15-27; 21:15-19). This showed Peter that his call remained and his position as a disciple was restored.

In the same way, God has redeemed women's power of influence, and it happened right where the original abuse of that power occurred—in a garden! Think of this, who was the first person Jesus encountered after his resurrection? Yes, it was Mary Magdalene . . . a woman (John 20:10-16)! Is that not fitting since the first sin was committed by a woman? The whole scene is so incredible. Look what Jesus did when they met. He gave Mary an assignment—to "go . . . and tell" (John 20:17).

There in the garden, Jesus, who is called "the last Adam" (1 Corinthians 15:45, 47), invited a woman to be a good influence. Jesus had previously told the disciples to meet him in Galilee after his resurrection (Matthew 28:10). Mary's job was to go to Jesus' disciples and encourage them—influence them—to *obey*. This was her opportunity to be a suitable helper. Jesus called her to strengthen the faith of those men, inspire them to rise to their full potential and to fulfill the original calls they had received from the Lord. In so doing, Jesus called her to fulfill the original role the Lord gave to women! Ladies, we're no longer under that curse. We're redeemed!

Use Your Power for Good

Now it's our turn. A moment ago, we looked at the ways a few guys responded to painful issues in their lives. Keep in mind that most of those guys were not openly expressing their feelings. In real life, we'd have no way of knowing what was happening behind the scenes. Based on what we normally would know or see, let's look at them one more time and find how—or if—we can be a positive influence on these guys. Is there still a way a girl can respond? Let's brainstorm.

• Bob's best friend, David, moved away.

Bob seems kind of lost when I see him in the halls now. I know he must miss David, but should I bring it up? I don't want to embarrass him. I guess I'll pray. Maybe if the right opportunity arises, I'll share how much I miss Dave. Then if Bob wants to talk about it, he'll know I can relate.

• Jacob's parents got divorced.

Jacob has lost weight lately. Mrs. Wells, our American lit teacher, frowned when she handed him his test results last Friday. He must not be doing too well. I'm gonna pray for him. I wonder if Mrs. Wells knows Jacob's parents were recently divorced. I'm not in his circle of friends, but maybe if I let her know, she can get him some help.

• Pete is small for his age.

(Rather than brainstorm on this one, I'm going to comment.) Guys who are small for their age, or who haven't started their growth spurt as soon as most other guys, suffer far more than girls could ever imagine. When girls are small, they're called *petite*. But guys suffer torturous ridicule from other guys if they're smaller in stature or are slower in going through puberty. Usually, even the guys who tease have no idea how deeply they're wounding a comrade because the smaller young man generally responds to the jesting by laughing and playing along.

Ladies, please never ever make comments to a guy about his being small or short. Even if he's a close friend. You may not mean any harm, but this is a topic for guys that is completely off-limits. Do not tease—even gently.

If a guy gets teased about his size in a mixed group, refuse to laugh along—even if the victim is laughing! It will speak volumes to him. And it will send an important message to the rest of the group as well. That's powerful influence, sister.

But don't pity him either. Remember, guys want respect. If a guy mentions his size in a conversation, you're being allowed into a very sacred part of his life. Don't patronize him by saying that sooner or later he'll grow. That's something you don't know. Share what you admire about him—his love of animals, his amazing speed on the soccer field, his generosity, etc. This lets him know that you see there's more to him than physical size. And it will help him see himself in a more balanced manner.

And do pray for him. Unless he's your literal brother, you will probably never see the anguish a guy suffers for being short. Maybe not even then; it's a very private matter for guys. But you can make a huge difference through prayer and sincere affirmation.

Giving respect and genuine compliments will help you see him in a more accurate light too. A guy's height is no measure of his masculinity.

• Joe's sister was in a serious skating accident.

I wonder how Joe's sister is doing. He looks so down. I think I'll ask him what hospital she's in so I can send a card. Maybe that will show I'm ready to listen if he wants to talk. And if he doesn't want to . . . well, at least he knows I care.

• Not only does Zach have a bad case of acne, he's moody and not as friendly as he used to be.

I freak whenever I break out! What must Zach be going through? No wonder he's moody and withdrawn. Everyone says we'll grow out of this but, hey, we live our lives one day at a time and today looks miserable for Zach. I think I'll ask him what his secret is to doing so well in biology.

• Steve is an all-star, but we never see his parents at games.

I wonder where Steve's parents are. I don't want to ask him, but it's gotta hurt that they're never around. My dad comes to all our games. I think I'll ask him to say a few friendly words to Steve next Friday when we play against Central High. I'm going to tell my youth pastor about Steve too. Steve needs a support group who love him for who he is, rather than just for what he does.

These are only a few ideas. Each situation for the guys in your life will be unique, but through prayer and careful thought you can discern how to be supportive and when that may mean to simply continue praying. It's now up to us to use our Girl Power for good. Think of it! You can change the world *because* you're a woman! Every time you see a guy's vulnerability, it's a divine opportunity to do that!

Secret No. 10

Guys Want to Be Heroes

Guys call them chick flicks—movies like *The Princess Bride, Ever After, The Princess Diaries* and *First Knight*—because girls love to watch them . . . over and over! Actually, it's not just movies. Certain books captivate too—timeless classics like *Cinderella, Sleeping Beauty* and *Snow White.*

Whether it's movies or books, the heroine is a princess (or eventually becomes one), and females of all ages love identifying with her. They dream of how exquisite it must feel to be a princess with glittering tiaras and gorgeous gowns, and they imagine attending grand balls, especially when there's a handsome prince involved.

Amid all this dreamy longing, guys roll their eyes and *pretend* to barely tolerate girls' romantic swooning. But ladies, you aren't the only ones who enjoy fantasizing. Guys have their own version of heroic characters that they love to identify with—what about Batman and

Spiderman for starters?

From the time they're little, guys picture themselves as brave knights, mighty hunters, courageous soldiers, sports stars and superheroes. And this doesn't stop when they become men. (Think James Bond!)

[All guys want to be heroes!]

At first, older girls may pooh-pooh the idea of being a princess, thinking they left that stage behind with their dollhouses and tea parties. But females don't outgrow their fantasies either. What about vying for homecoming queen and entering beauty pageants? There's just something about a sparkling tiara and meeting Prince Charming . . .

[
So if girls love the idea of being a princess whisked away by a handsome prince, and guys dig the idea of being a superhero who rescues and wins the fair maiden, it makes a great plan for everyone, right?
]

It's a fantastic plan . . . fun, romantic, rewarding . . . and meaningful! (Its origins may surprise you; we'll look at that later.)

But for most of us, the princess-hero plan has been muddled by our culture. Many young ladies don't realize they *are* potential "princesses." They have never learned to appreciate their femininity. In fact, they've been taught just the opposite, to strive to be like guys. So girls feel guilty about being feminine.

One mother related that her daughter and her daughter's friends balked at an opportunity to attend an event that was planned especially for the girls of their youth group. The evening was designed around the theme of being a princess. The girls thought the idea of being a princess seemed silly, immature and fictitious. They had no intention of attending! When I recounted this conversation to another young lady, she told me she too had chosen to not go—for the same reason!

It is not at all uncommon for girls today to draw back from things that seem too girlish (emphasis on the *ish*)! After all, they've been raised to be strong, independent and to have an I'm-just-as-good-as-the-guys mentality.

Though they've been taught this attitude, there resides inside each girl a stirring—a certain discontent—and it's unsettling because girls are discovering that their princess within is yearning to come out. Ladies, that's not something to fear, deny or feel guilty about. It's something to embrace! Every girl who belongs to the Lord Jesus *is* a princess. God never intended for that to be programmed out of you. You have full permission to rediscover that you—his daughter—are indeed a princess!

A Princess?

Being a princess does not mean that you're better than other people, but it does have notable significance. First, it means that you have more privileges because daughters of kings naturally have special status. They have direct access to the king and to all the benefits that go along with being part of his household.

Second, it means that you have more responsibility. Duty is important in the role of a princess.

> As the daughter of the King of kings,
> you're expected to represent him properly
> and care about what concerns him.

"With privilege comes responsibility." I'm sure you've heard *that* before!

And third, it means that there is quite likely a "prince" somewhere out there searching for you!

So how does a princess act? What are the qualities of a young maiden that catch the eye of a prince and make a guy today want to be a superhero?

Nobility

A princess is noble. Remember the princess in *First Knight*? Her nobility was displayed through several traits.

Posture

She was a young lady who carried herself with poise and dignity.

The princess stood straight and walked gracefully. I've watched guys watch girls. They notice girls with good posture. OK, they more than notice—they stare at girls who have stately bearing! To guys, it's a stunning attribute of beauty. One guy exclaimed, "Good posture is a big thing—huge thing!"

Even if you feel uncomfortably tall, stand straight. Be regal. Don't allow yourself to feel apologetic about your height. Keep in mind that being taller than your guy friends may be temporary. Guys often get their growth spurts in their upper teen years, long after most girls have reached their adult height. Don't spoil your posture by stooping or slumping.

> Short guys and tall girls get picked on by inconsiderate peers. Ignore it. God doesn't make mistakes.

There are (or depending on your age, *will* be) plenty of guys who prefer tall girls. And all guys admire poise. Try it and see for yourself!

Stand straight too if you feel exceptionally short, not with the intent of trying to make yourself look taller, but with the admirable bearing of a princess. Lots of guys adore petite girls. I have seen a number of shorter-than-average girls who had excellent posture and moved with such grace that guys were nearly in awe of them.

Listening

Another aspect of being noble is to listen attentively. A princess looks directly at the person speaking and gives him her full focus. She doesn't glance around the room looking for someone more interesting. Because she offers undivided attention, she makes people feel special. And that's what makes *her* special!

Character and Duty

When the princess in *First Knight* spoke, she chose her words carefully. She exercised control over her emotions and made choices based on what she knew was right rather than on how she felt. She faced temptations and repeatedly made choices that revealed her strength of character. Though she wasn't perfect, she possessed a strong sense of duty which came with knowing she was a princess. Her noble behavior won the hearts of the people and inspired a swashbuckling rogue to become noble as well.

Selflessness

A princess thinks of others. In the film *Ever After*, the poor farm wench displayed selflessness when the prince tossed her some silver coins in exchange for the use of her horse. Instead of taking the money for herself, she used the coins to redeem an elderly man who had been sold into slavery. Though this young lady was not yet officially a princess, she exhibited the qualities of one. And her selfless act brought her once again across the path of the prince!

Humility

Another princess virtue is humility. A princess does not demand or expect special treatment from others. She chooses to refrain from bragging or calling attention to herself. Instead she focuses on others and their needs. She doesn't need to be in the spotlight because she already knows she's a princess.

There's a beautiful dignity in humility.

> When you know who you are (a princess with all your strengths *and* weaknesses), when you know your worth in God and your purpose, you won't need to be—or dare to be—proud.

You don't have to compare yourself with others or act defensive. You're free simply to live and walk in your identity with a quiet peace that makes pride unnecessary.

A princess's humility also shows as she seeks and accepts advice and counsel. She is teachable. She doesn't think she knows everything or has all the answers. One of the most exciting examples of this is in the book of Esther in the Bible. (Here we go looking at Esther again. Talk about power of influence; after thousands of years she's *still* impacting people!)

It was Esther's willingness to seek advice that placed her in the coveted position of queen. As queen she continued to humble herself by listening to the counsel of her elder cousin, who raised her. This attitude eventually saved her life and the lives of her people. It's a fabulous story of drama, excitement and romance. And it's true!

Kindness

A princess is extraordinarily beneficent. Gentle, generous, compassionate, patient, good-natured, forgiving—all these beautiful words describe a princess. Remember Snow White's gentleness as she sang among the birds and animals? And her soothing sense of humor in dealing with the shenanigans of the seven dwarfs?

When Cinderella was mistreated, she did not become mean-spirited or vindictive. She didn't try to get even, but patiently endured. Though she shed tears, we know Cinderella's virtue was rewarded when her wish to attend the ball was granted.

Trust and Faithfulness

A princess believes and trusts. In *The Princess Bride*, even when her hero was gone and all hope looked lost, the maiden continued to believe he would return. Her faith was severely tested by ill-intentioned people who lied about her hero. If she had chosen to believe them, she would have lost everything. But she trusted, and her prince eventually did return and rescue her. Several times!

Getting back to Cinderella, look what happened in the midst of her exciting time at the ball. She was tested even further by having to leave the dance and the arms of the prince in order to be faithful to a promise. But a princess is a princess regardless of her attire or her circumstances. Even what appeared to be the end of her dream couldn't hold back her destiny. The day came when Cinderella's foot once again fit into the glass slipper held by the prince!

Occupied

A princess doesn't sit around twiddling her thumbs, waiting for a prince to come on the scene. She stays occupied! She has vision, purpose and direction. She has a life of her own.

> A princess finds her prince—or perhaps I should say the prince finds *her*—while she is going about her Father's business.

If a princess is living her life looking for the prince, then she's not likely to run across him, because *he'll* be in the center of *his* Father's business. Sitting around waiting won't put you in the spot where the prince can find you. You must be in the right place at the right time so your paths will cross!

I was well into my twenties when I felt the call to become a missionary. As much as I longed to serve the Lord, I had mixed feelings about facing four years of Bible college. In my mind, that meant I was taking myself out of circulation as far as marriage was concerned. But I went anyway, all four years. It wasn't until I was on the mission field that I met the prince who was to become my husband. The irony was that he and I were from the same church! Because it was a large church, our paths didn't cross . . . until I was hundreds of miles away . . . and until he gave up a fishing vacation to go on a missions trip instead! Our paths met only when both of us gave up our own agendas to serve our Father's purposes.

Every chick flick verifies the principle of being occupied. A girl with vision and purpose exudes mystery. (You know by now how much guys love that.) A girl occupied with life tantalizes a guy's curiosity. He wants to know what makes her tick. The princess who is occupied is an attractive challenge!

Respect and Admiration

A princess doesn't compete with the prince. On the contrary, she builds him up. It is her admiration and respect that inspire the prince and compel him to greatness. When he sees that he is a hero in her eyes, it's no wonder he's willing to suffer for her. A hero will go through anything to keep an admiring princess by his side!

A Hero?

Yes! Guys want to be heroes—*especially* in the eyes of females! It's been a costly mistake for women to take away that privilege from guys! Young ladies have been taught to no longer acknowledge a need or express a desire to be rescued or protected by guys. Woe to the poor fellow who tries to open a door for a female! Instead of being appreciated, he's given a shriveling look accompanied by an "I can do it myself" retort.

It goes further. "Not only do we not need you guys, we can do everything you can do—and better!" Females set out to prove this by competing with guys. We already talked about this in Guys vs. Girls, but we didn't look at the consequences as they relate to the hero side of guys—and it's a big deal!

With their independent stance, women have shut men out and shut them off. Guys' attempts at chivalry have been rebuffed so often that they've grown discouraged with the idea.

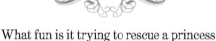

> What fun is it trying to rescue a princess
> who wants to be the prince?

Girls miss out when they thwart guys' desires to direct their bravado toward the benefit of ladies. They miss out on the respect and reverence that men used to reserve for females. And they lose a large measure of guys' interest.

(Aah, but this is not so for princesses. In this day and age, they stand out! As a young lady who maintains her virtue, you are rarer, more precious and even more desirable!)

Being a hero is deeply ingrained in a guy. Laws haven't changed their hearts or quelled their desire to perform daring feats. Guys will do mighty stunts whether or not it's for the sake of females.

So what does today's guy do with his desire to be a hero? This is where the upsurge in extreme sports comes in. Even though guys may not do it consciously, I believe a big reason they delve into these over-the-top activities is because the more traditional and romantic outlets for their energies have been shut down through insults and competition from women. By invading a man's world and insisting on "equality," females have taken themselves out of the picture as precious to guys. A girl who is one of the guys is boring to males, so they expand their world and move on to other pursuits. And extreme sports are still mainly a guy's pastime.

This is disturbing. Have women unknowingly pushed guys to endanger their lives needlessly in order for them to maintain their unique identities as males? There's no question that many guys are into extreme sports because they think they're fun. But I can't help but question whether a lot of the interest in life-threatening sports comes for other reasons too. Subconscious reasons.

Guys want to lay down their lives for a valid cause. From the beginning, this cause has centered on duty to God and country and on protecting and providing for their families. We see an example of this in 1 Samuel 30. When the Amalekites ravaged the camp of David, they stole everything, including the wives and children of the future king and all his men. Now that was a valid cause! Along with his band of mighty warriors, David pursued the enemy relentlessly until they recovered everything and everyone!

With women telling guys "we want to be equal with you," they've taken away guys' reasons for being protectors and conquerors. But guys will always be heroes at heart, and they can't help but protest when that passion is extinguished by the very ones they long to protect—and impress!

Women have misunderstood men's motives. Can I let you in on an especially endearing secret about guys? When women want to take roles that traditionally belong to males, sometimes the reason men resist is not at all because men want to hold women back! If you could think like a guy, you'd discover their motives have been honorable.

[God built it into men to be conquerors, protectors and providers.]

When women try to fill those roles, it makes guys feel *guilty!* To protect and provide is so inherent in a guy's nature that they view women filling men's roles as a sign that they are not carrying out their responsibilities to care for women! They don't want to allow females to do certain things because they feel to do so is to shirk their God-given mandate to protect and provide. It's a heroic mindset.

In today's culture, this puts guys into yet another no-win situation. Their hearts tell them one thing, but society has tried programming them to believe something else. When men step aside so women may do things that men see as roles for males, guys feel guilty because it says to them that they're failing. Yet if they *don't* allow women to do these things, they're condemned for repressing women, and they feel guilty for that too!

Guys are torn between obeying God and obeying man. The Bible says that men are to treat women as the weaker partner (1 Peter 3:7). But women are telling guys, "Don't you dare!"

To be sure, many guys throughout the ages have used the Scriptures or their physical strength to abuse women and treat them as inferior.

In some parts of the world, entire cultures oppress women. We can't ignore this. It's been a major cause for women rising up in rebellion.

The Original Princess Story

What a sorry mess we've made out of the whole prince-princess plan. We've forgotten, or perhaps never knew, that it is patterned after the greatest story of them all—the account of Prince Jesus rescuing his bride-to-be, the church! *This* is the *original* prince and princess story! What's even more exciting, it's no fairy tale. It's the gospel truth! And it does indeed end with a promised life of happily ever after! How incredible is that!

No wonder we have a fascination with such stories. Our spirits are bearing witness with the Lord's original plan. That longing to be a princess is your spirit desiring to be united with the Prince.

> The longing guys have to be heroes is a reflection of God's heart for his bride the church, to pursue, rescue and win her.

Jesus is our original hero! He literally went through Hell to rescue his bride. Jesus, our original knight in shining armor, will indeed come back for his princess, and he'll even be riding a white horse (Revelation 19:11-16)! He also told her to stay occupied until he arrives (Luke 19:13, KJV). Then he will take his bride to be with him forever in a home that glistens with jewels (Revelation 21:10-21).

Can you imagine telling Jesus that you're able to do just fine by yourself, that you don't want to be or need to be rescued? Imagine telling him you're just as good as he and want to be equal with him. (Do you remember what happened when Satan tried that? Check out Isaiah 14:12-15; Ezekiel 28:12-19; Luke 10:18; 1 Timothy 3:6.)

Can you see how it spoils God's pattern when females reject the chivalry of men? Part of the fun of being a princess is to be treated like one. When a prince finds you, don't spoil the fun (or the pattern) by competing with him. Let the prince be the hero! Maybe that's not the right way to say it. We shouldn't "let" the prince be the hero; we need to *recognize* him as the hero!

More Qualities of a Princess

So, are you saying that we princesses have to pretend to be weak just so we can be "rescued"? I'm so glad you asked! There are qualities of a princess that we haven't covered yet. And one of them, believe it or not, is strength!

Strength

A princess is strong! Of course this applies to character. We saw that in the princess from *First Knight*, the strength she exhibited as she resisted temptations and made tough choices based on duty. And we certainly see it in Esther! It took tremendous strength of character to risk her life by approaching the king when he didn't request her presence (Esther 4:11-16).

But a princess may be strong physically also. She doesn't have to pretend to be fragile in order to appear feminine. Take Cinderella for example. With all the hard labor she was forced to do, there's no way that princess-to-be could have been a weakling!

And what about Rebekah in the Bible? She was chosen as a wife for Abraham's son, Isaac, which meant that she married into a wealthy family. But do you have any idea what the qualifications were for being his wife? She had to be willing and able to draw enough water to quench the thirst of ten camels! Ladies, that's a lot of hard work! (Check out Genesis 24:1-66). Included in the profile of a wife of noble character is this description: "She sets about her work vigorously; her arms are strong for her tasks" (Proverbs 31:17).

Not all girls can be a Rebekah. Some girls must live with physical challenges. But a princess is not a couch potato! She does what she is able to keep her mind and body as healthy as possible.

Authenticity

There is a big variety of guys, but few are looking for a Miss Priss or an Amazon. One guy explained it this way: "I don't wanna have to baby-sit her." (That would be a Miss Priss, the girl who won't do anything for herself.) While he wants to be the hero, he wants his girl to be competent.

Another guy said, "I don't want someone that can beat me up!" *(Laughter.)* "Well, I don't!" *(More laughter.)* (That would be the Amazon—bigger, stronger, smarter.) Obviously he doesn't want to be overwhelmed by a girl's abilities.

Much of a guy's perception of a girl depends on her motive, which generally shows through her conduct. Using phony helplessness to get a guy's attention is a turnoff, likewise acting clueless and ditzy. It can get tiresome for a guy to have to do everything for a girl. Guys goof off with such girls, but they rarely take them seriously.

On the other hand, guys do love to be magnanimous. A guy is showing respect for you and extending courtesy when he offers his assistance. (Note: When being approached by a stranger, you must use extreme caution. That's a different issue entirely, and that's not what I'm talking about here.)

Suppose you have a flat tire on your car. Bravo for you if you know how and are able to change it. But when a guy (dad, brother, friend, boyfriend, etc.) presents himself to help, it doesn't impress him when you insist on wielding your own wrench. You'll just seem proud. Your decline of his help reads as rejection. And you've just denied him the pleasure of being a hero. Wouldn't it be more fun to fix that tire together or to keep him company while he helps out?

> Being a hero has to do with being useful, helpful, productive and protective—it's about what guys *do.*

Guys feel valued when they can be of service to you.

Intelligence

Be real with your smarts too. Intelligence and wisdom are desirable qualities in a princess. Guys don't want girls to hide their intelligence (just don't flaunt it). They enjoy having a good conversation with a girl. One college guy put it like this: "I like a girl who can carry on a conversation covering current events, not current styles."

Remember the fifteen-year-old guy in Secret No. 2 who said basically the same thing? Even at his age, guys value a girl who can hold her own in a discussion—without being argumentative!

Are you seeing an underlying theme in all these tips?

The secret is in how a girl makes a guy feel about himself!

I can't emphasize this enough. Guys want to be heroes! The girl who knows how to make a guy feel like a hero is likely to have her pick of several princes! If you catch the full importance, you will never again want to say or do anything to make a guy feel depreciated.

Ellie was interested in Hayden. She was fairly certain that he was interested in her too. (And, in fact, he was!) But she felt frustrated with him and grew impatient because he wasn't making overtures toward her according to *her* timetable. To prod him along a bit, Ellie teased Hayden about his reticence. She meant to encourage him to be more outgoing, but her choice of words made him pull away like a hermit crab into its shell.

Her approach didn't make him feel good inside. He was already struggling to get up the nerve to ask her out, so Ellie's chiding made him feel disgusted with himself. No guy wants to be around a girl who makes him feel like a loser. Ellie had no intention of hurting Hayden, but she didn't understand the importance of how a girl can affect the view a guy has of himself.

[
Guys are powerfully attracted to girls
who build a guy's self-confidence.
]

Forget the fake flattery though; they can see through it. Genuine affirmation and admiration, however, are powerful motivators for guys!

Think of how much guys enjoy cheerleaders. These edifying females aren't a modern day idea, you know. We find cheerleaders way back in the Old Testament! Perhaps Moses' sister Miriam was the first. With tambourine in hand, she led the women of Israel in songs and dancing after the Red Sea closed over their pursuing enemies (Exodus 15:20, 21).

Then there's the story of King Saul and David. They were surrounded by cheerleaders! Saul had an entire kingdom of wealth and honor, yet when the Israelite women sang "Saul has slain his thousands, and David his tens of thousands," he seethed with jealousy (1 Samuel 18:5-9). David, a mere commoner, a shepherd boy, was the guy who received the praises of the women! In spite of all that he had, King Saul felt like less of a hero when compared to him. He became obsessed with unseating his lowly rival, all because David had the admiration of the women!

Yes indeed, guys are powerfully influenced by how you make them feel about themselves.

Let's reflect for a moment on the value the Lord places on our praise. We can learn something from the similarities between our original Prince and guys today. Now we know that our views of God do not change his view of himself, so that's not a similarity. But in the psalms alone, we are admonished repeatedly to praise the Lord. Prince Jesus wants to hear the praises of his bride, the church! When she believes in him and praises him, he is released to do mighty works!

Conversely, when we withhold our praise, it hinders what he wants to do for us. Jesus did not do many mighty works in his hometown because of the unbelief of the people there (Matthew 13:54-58). That hometown was a "princess" who would not believe in him and could not be rescued by him. Unwillingness to acknowledge and praise him resulted in little enjoyment of him.

The parallel, of course, is that . . .

[
We cripple guys with our negative words
and attitudes toward them.
]

We'll neither enjoy them nor receive much from them if we withhold our admiration. But young ladies willing to encourage and edify guys will reap the benefits.

God loves the cheering of his bride! We're even told that God inhabits the praises of his people (Psalm 22:3, KJV). What an awesome thought! Praise draws his presence!

That's true for guys too. If you praise guys, it's gonna draw their presence! They'll want to be around you. Sometimes a girl's devotion is what keeps a guy alive, literally. Think of the value a soldier places on the woman in his life—mother, wife, fiancée or girlfriend—wherever he goes, he takes her photo with him. She is his link to reality, his reason for being a hero.

But it's not just soldiers. In life-threatening situations, many a guy has endured unimaginable circumstances, spurred on solely by the hope of seeing his ladylove and family again. Women are the inspiration of men!

Cheering a guy on doesn't have to be just for boyfriends either. You can bring out the hero in your dad, brother(s) and friends just as well. All males thrive on the encouragement and admiration of females.

Guys give women an astonishing amount of power over them. It all has to do with how you make a guy feel about himself. If he feels like a hero around you, you will be precious to him. Grasp this secret and you can change the lives of countless guys! And it might entirely change your life!

Secret No. 11

❦

Guys Notice Homemaking Skills

The way to a guy's heart is through chocolate chip cookies. *Homemade* chocolate chip cookies, that is! If there's ever a time when guys are in tune to food, it's during their growth-spurt and college years. Young men are absolute eating machines at this age, and kudos to the young lady who knows how to cook! To guys, she's a priceless treasure. How do I know? I've heard it.

Sitting around our kitchen table, heartily munching on my fare, guys discuss which girls can cook and which can't. Between mouthfuls of barbecue meatballs, they rave about girls—by name—whom they know can prepare a tasty meal. Picture a conversation something like this:

"Sheri makes some incredible lasagna!" Alec says with a grin.

"Her sister Misty's an awesome cook too!" Mike pipes in.

Stabbing another meatball, Nate gives his two cents worth. "Well, you can see why . . . look at their mom! Mrs. Baker is always having kids over and she is a goooood cook!"

"Yeah," Mike agrees, "but, in our whole youth group, who else do you know that could fix a meal?" He shakes his fork for emphasis. "I can't think of another girl."

"Uh . . ."

"Well . . ."

Silence.

"Wait a minute!" Until then, Cooper had only been listening. "Every time we have cell group, Darcy brings them gooey chocolate brownies!"

"Dude!" Alec laughs. "I have to fight to get one!"

Mike presses his point, "But man shall not live by brownies alone. What about real food?"

Silence again.

Nate breaks their contemplation. "Well, what about the girls at school?"

"Forget that!"

The guys look at each other and laugh nervously.

"Man . . .we're in trouble!"

Yes, guys are more than willing to brag on girls who have impressed them with their culinary abilities. But they also laugh, uneasily, about how rare these girls seem to be.

Believe it or not, in these days of liberation, guys still notice a girl's homemaking skills. In fact, the older my sons and their friends become, the more alert they are to the presence or lack of those skills in their female friends. *Can she cook? Administrate? Is she kind to children? How does she handle money?* And more important, *Does she care to learn?*

Domestic know-how seems to be in danger of becoming a lost art. And guys are in a bit of a panic.

[
A girl may be hot to look at,

but how cool is she in the kitchen?
]

In their more rational moments, especially while a bunch of those guys are sitting around eating a mom's homemade chili, guys realize there's got to be more to a girl than the way she looks.

They ladle portions of the steaming concoction into bowls, toss on some shredded cheese and then, as they discuss one of their favorite topics—girls—between scoops of chili and bites of cornbread, it suddenly dawns on them that their days of eating home cooking are close to an end. Unless they can find a wife to take over. That's when the guys panic because they know almost no girls who could fill the bill, and they're well aware that cherry-flavored lip gloss on their favorite girl just isn't gonna suffice.

Can She Cook?

It seems that few of today's girls can cook, and maybe one reason is because they're growing up in homes where many of their mothers know little about it. For the past couple of generations, being just a mom was something women admitted to only in a low tone of voice and with lots of guilt. Household talents were put on a low rung of the ladder to success. Now we're reaping the consequences of that mindset.

Today's meals often consist of food that is fast, frozen or fake.

Prepackaged mixes list ingredients that most of us can't pronounce. We gobble it down on the run and assume the next generation will be just as capable of reading directions on a box.

I confess, there've been days when I too left my sons to fend for themselves. Knowing I wouldn't be home one day, I left a short note on the counter for our guys with a can of baked beans. Hot dogs were in the freezer. It couldn't get much simpler than that, I thought.

When I returned home later that evening, I spotted the remains of a pan of made-from-scratch cornbread sitting on the kitchen counter. It had been carefully covered with plastic wrap. Next to the pan sat the unopened can of baked beans.

"Why didn't you guys eat the beans?" I asked the next morning. I was definitely perplexed. "I tried to make it easy for you."

"Oh, I didn't know how to fix the beans," my son said matter-of-factly, "so I made cornbread."

I didn't know whether to laugh or cry. I'd failed miserably at teaching my sons instant meal tricks, but our guys were obviously picking up pointers from me in the kitchen. To this day, the son in charge of their supper that night makes a better pan of cornbread than I!

Still, he and plenty of other guys lament over lack of proficiency in the kitchen by females. "It's not just a concern of the guys at church," my son exclaims, "even the guys at school (university) talk about it!" In a conversation among guys sitting out on our patio this past weekend, one of their friends brought up the topic again.

I'm telling you, guys notice homemaking skills! Have you any idea what a find you'll be if you develop a knack for cooking and domestic management? You will be a prize! Or to quote my son, "She'll be a gold mine!"

Instead of being looked upon as shallow, guys will see you as a girl who is developing herself into a young lady—so liberated—that she dares to openly enjoy homemaking!

Guys can't help but celebrate. When a girl feels at home in the kitchen, it's easier for a guy to see his own potential—as a hero. In essence it gives him permission to go ahead and be a guy without worrying about confusion of roles. I know that's a touchy subject, but it's time for girls to shake off the guilt that too many of them feel when their domestic genes overrule their training to compete with guys.

For years, women have been so busy looking at what guys do, and then trying to match them, that mastering and excelling at domestic skills have gone by the wayside. That's not your fault. You're growing up in a culture where you continuously hear about the limitless possibilities and potential for girls. That's great. But a major part of the possibilities picture has been left out lately. You haven't been hearing about the fulfillment—or the power—that comes with being a homemaker!

A woman has different seasons in her life.

> In Proverbs 31 we see that praiseworthy women
> handle real estate, run businesses, teach, do charity
> work and are diligent workers. It's all in there.
> So is being a wife and mother.

It's a major portion—but that part about being a keeper of the home has been largely ignored for the past few generations.

If your foremost desire is to be a stay-at-home wife and mother, don't think for one minute that you are selling yourself short as a female. You're not betraying your gender, and it's neither a lowly nor a lesser calling. It's also not taking the easy route! That stirring is from the Lord! He wants to redeem, restore and release the homemaking gifts in young ladies again.

I don't think anyone needs to tell you that today's families are falling apart. For their preservation, it is absolutely essential that girls feel free to delight in and embrace the domestic nature of their femininity. It's with God's blessing that you nurture that part of your "nesting instincts." It will most certainly draw the praise of guys!

Where Do I Start?

I think I'd better say here that if you haven't learned to sew, cook and clean, it's not all your mom's fault either. My mother was a stay-at-home mom. She was a homemaker par excellence. She sewed, canned, cooked, and baked cookies, pies, rolls, donuts and bread (no bread machines in those days), while managing our household and raising eight children. She never worked outside our home until we kids were grown.

As I grew up, I had the privilege of observing all the traditional tasks of a housewife. I could have learned everything, but I was too busy thinking about boys. Oh, I picked up quite a bit, but it took a few years before I made the necessary connection between my fascination with guys and my needing to actually use those homemaking skills. By then, I wished I'd paid a lot more attention!

You're never too young or too old to begin learning to be a homemaker. I saw this as a single missionary when I had the privilege of visiting a family in a remote village that could be reached only by flying in.

Our aircraft's pontoons touched down on the lake, and we taxied across the water to a dock where our host's fourteen-year-old son helped his dad secure the little bush plane with ropes. I was impressed by the calm maturity and skill of the young man. There was yet more to impress me.

Inside the home, while the mother tended to other tasks, the nine-year-old daughter was busy making bread! I was challenged. I'd grown up on home-baked bread. Time and again I had watched my mother knead and form loaves. I'd been there to sample slices cut from a loaf still steaming from the oven—we vied for the crispy end pieces—but I'd never asked her to teach me. When I saw what that little girl could do, something began rising in my own heart. Someday, I told myself, I would master the art of bread making.

That opportunity came just a few years later when, as a new bride, I found myself living in a remote village! We were 150 miles from the nearest city, in a little house with no running water. (Our "bathroom" was an outhouse with a luxurious foam seat. We crafted that after discovering foam was much warmer than plywood when the temperature was forty degrees below! Oh, but that's another story. . . .)

Our home was heated with a wood stove and we hauled our water from the train station. But we had one convenience—electricity—and I had an electric range! It was amid those rustic circumstances that a dear friend in the village, well versed in the feminine arts of homemaking, taught me to make bread.

What a wonderful satisfaction, to gaze upon those beautifully browned loaves as the aroma of bread, fresh from the oven, filled our little home. I was hooked! And in the days and years that followed, my husband and sons were hooked on devouring it!

Be a Kitchen Apprentice

Contrary to how it may sound, living in the sticks is not a requirement for learning homemaking. Maybe your mother doesn't do a lot of "from scratch" meal preparation. You can still learn. Sign up for some home economics or family living classes in school. Or pray and ask the Lord to give you a homemaking mentor. It might be an aunt, a grandmother, a neighbor or someone in your church. Most women who enjoy being home keepers are thrilled to pass on their tips to interested young women!

When you find a willing mentor, you might want to consider asking her to teach a small group of girls. Form a club! Think of the possibilities. Once you've mastered a few of the basics, you and your friends can plan and prepare an entire meal. Then choose a few worthy guys and invite them to sample what you've learned. I doubt you'll have any trouble finding guys willing to do a taste test (as long as you don't tell them it's your first meal ever)!

Since you're doing it as a group, no girl has to feel that her individual culinary techniques are on trial. Though, if your contribution is a smashing success, you'll likely want the accolades! And guys are resilient (as well as always hungry), so regardless of the outcome of your first meal, I'm guessing they'll be more than happy to be invited to sample your efforts again. And again!

How About Her Housekeeping?

By any chance, does the term *housekeeping* make you squirm a little when you glance around your own bedroom? OK, how do you feel when your mother suggests you help her with straightening the house? Well . . . um . . .

[
Who do you think is going to maintain the castle

when you're living happily ever after?
]

Isn't your knight in shining armor going to be busy slaying dragons at the office, or wherever?

Keeping a neat home doesn't have to be drudgery. After all, your living quarters are where you get to express your personality and creativity. But that decor isn't going to look its best if you don't know how to keep it neat and clean. Dust bunnies aren't as cute as their name sounds! As well as being a matter of aesthetics, a clean and tidy home (and room!) is a health issue.

If you're eager to learn, God will supply resources for your domestic education. To earn pocket money as a girl, I helped an elderly lady with household chores. It was from her I learned how to form "envelope corners" when making a bed.

The majority of my education in household cleaning skills came— of all places—while I was in Bible college! All students worked on the school campus to help cover tuition. Among my varied assignments, I spent two years on the cleaning crew. I learned plenty, thanks to Annie, a godly role model on staff, who loved the Lord and loved us students. She had an incredible handle on cleaning and hospitality.

I confess there were days, such as while I scoured the guys' dorm bathrooms, when I felt like Cinderella. There were several of us Cinderellas. One day, my cleaning partner and I came across another "scullery maid" lying faceup on the tile floor in the guys' shower room. She was simply too grossed out to scrub. It was hilarious. A sense of humor worked wonders to keep us going. Tears of laughter were more therapeutic than tears of self-pity and they were a lot more fun.

But I too had moments when woe-is-me thoughts came knocking. One such instance arrived while I frantically raced to clean an entire ladies' room in fifteen minutes. Tears of frustration stung my eyes when suddenly I "heard" a gentle thought, "You can quit if you want to, you know." The Lord was telling me I really did have a choice. I could choose an easier route if I wished. I'm so glad I determined to stick it out because I didn't realize at the time that we Cinderellas were really attending princess school!

Is She Kind to Children?

Knowing how to cook, clean and raise children doesn't need to be, and probably shouldn't be, the *only* focus in your life. After all, raising children does eventually come to an end; the time will come when your children will be grown and out of the nest. But while you're thinking about life with Prince Charming, you're not likely to be thinking about that happily-ever-*after-the-children* season. So while you hone your homemaking skills, don't feel you must forsake your other talents and interests. The best approach is not to overlook either stage and to prepare for both.

Right now though, like you, guys are looking at the earlier stages of their potentially happily-ever-after life. Those years are critically important, not just for the guys' sake but because, as a couple, you will be modeling a lifestyle that your children will emulate when *they* become adults!

Are you getting this?

> Guys aren't looking for girls with homemaking abilities just so the guys can live a cushy life. Yes, they're taking stock of what kind of wife a girl will be, but they're also considering what sort of mother she'll be for their children!

Guys notice how a girl acts around kids. Is she kind? Does she enjoy being with and caring for little ones? Is she patient? How does she treat her younger siblings?

Ouch! That last question is a tough one. Treating a younger brother or sister with compassion isn't usually as easy as being nice to someone who isn't in your immediate family. But how you treat those closest to you actually says the most about you!

In front of your friends, it might not feel cool to show kindness and respect to a younger sibling, especially if that brother or sister does stuff that embarrasses you. But it is, in fact, very cool not only to refrain from sarcasm and disdain but also to extend warmth and compassion to your family. Your friends will respect you more if you do.

Guys may never say anything, but when they see your cheerful and loving attitude toward siblings, you can be sure they take note. And the impression you leave lasts long after that moment. You see, you're giving clues as to what kind of a mother you will be.

In the lives of guys, your power of influence isn't limited to your dad, brothers, friends and husband. It will become powerfully active in your role as a mother! Guys received their first impressions of females from their mothers. Likewise, your son's first impression of women will come from you! A boy begins forming his attitudes about girls—and about himself—through his relationship with his mom. Being a godly mother to a son is foundational. It can influence the rest of his life *and* everyone whom his life touches! Inherently, guys realize at least some of this when they watch a girl relate with children.

[
What world-changing power God gives to mothers—for good or bad!
]

You needn't be rich or famous to make a lasting impact. Think of Moses' mother. She was a slave in Egypt, not exactly a prestigious position. In order to spare her son's life, she placed him in a basket and hid it among the bulrushes of the Nile River. You probably know the story of how Pharaoh's daughter discovered the infant, adopted him and named him Moses. His real mother was brought to Pharaoh's daughter who turned him back over to her to nurse. After he was weaned, Moses' mother had to give him back to Pharaoh's daughter, but her influence in those short years laid the foundations of Moses' life, his identity and his destiny (Exodus 2:1-10).

Through Moses the Israelites were led out of 400 years of slavery in Egypt. By his intercession they were spared from annihilation, and because of his devotion to the Lord, they—and *we*—received the first five books of the Bible, including the Ten Commandments! No small influence for a mother!

A mother's influence is just as critical when raising daughters. Your daughters will learn their first attitudes toward males from you. Your cheerfulness, reverence, admiration, support, cooperation, encouragement and respect toward your husband will set the example for your daughter(s). Knowing how influential females are in the lives of guys tells you how important your influence is in your daughter's life—it's world-changing—because she'll be influencing the next generation of guys!

Herodias is a frightening example of a mother's negative influence on her daughter. You can find the whole account in Matthew 14:3-11 and Mark 6:17-28. This mother had a grudge against John the Baptist because he preached against her sin and that of her husband, Herod, who just happened to also be her brother-in-law! Herodias couldn't do anything about her grudge because Herod, her unlawful husband, knew that John the Baptist was a holy man and he feared him. Herod was also intrigued by what John preached; he liked to listen to him.

One day there was a big birthday bash for Herod, and Herodias's daughter, who was the main entertainment, performed a dance for her uncle/stepdad and his guests. It must have been a doozy because he and the other partiers were so impacted that he promised to give her anything she asked—up to half his kingdom!

What do I mean by "doozy"? Her dance must have been extremely seductive. Well, do *you* think Herod would have been moved to give away half his empire if the girl had been clogging?

Herod had already put his salvation in jeopardy for a woman. Now he was putting his kingdom on the line as well, all because of the influence of the two main women in his household.

Herodias's daughter went right to her mother for advice on what to request. Then she returned to the king and, reflecting her mother's attitude, asked for the head of John the Baptist on a large platter. Herod, bound by his oath and his pride, reluctantly complied. The head was delivered to his stepdaughter who promptly presented it to her mother.

Ugh! What a grizzly story. But sadly true. That mother multiplied her wicked influence and stole a prophet from the entire world—all through her daughter! No small influence for a mother!

Is it any wonder that guys observe a girl's way with children?

How Does She Handle Money?

Not too long ago I overheard a guy tell our sons, "I'm not going after a girl till I can afford one. Right now I can hardly support myself, let alone a girl!"

> The closer guys get to the age for marriage, the more conscious they are of money and their ability to support a wife and family.

This means they also pay more attention to a girl's outlook on finances. They start asking questions like these:

- Does she have any credit cards?
- Is she in debt?
- What is her source of income? (parents, a job or both?)
- What is her attitude when she approaches her parents for money?
- Is she covetous?
- Does she have to have the best of everything?
- Does she take care of what she already has?
- Is she a grateful person?
- Is she content?

- Is she generous?
- How do her attitudes about money affect her outlook on guys?
- Does she gravitate toward the guys who seem to have the most money, the ritziest cars?
- As a wife, will she demand going into debt in order to have everything new when we start our home?

These are tough questions that could at first make you feel defensive. But they're practical and necessary issues that both guys *and* girls need to look at before marriage. You need to ask similar questions about any guy you're interested in. As a wife and mother, you'll want the assurance of knowing that your husband can handle money wisely.

A guy wants to bless his wife and make her happy. From his perspective, it's a red flag if a girl seems content only when she's getting some new bauble. This tells him she'll be a demanding and difficult-to-please partner. It goes back to that issue of how a girl makes a guy feel about himself. He doesn't want his worth in her eyes measured by how many material possessions he can provide for her. He doesn't want to feel that he must "earn" her favor. It's not just about money; it's about looking for a friend with whom to share his life. It's about trust and genuine love.

Do you know that guys actually discuss this issue? They wonder how they'll find a wife if they're financially prosperous.

> They question how they can be sure a girl will love a guy for who he is and not for his income. And they wonder if she'd stick with him if they went through hard times.

This is an area in which guys' vulnerability shows. Guys see so much money-grabbing in the world that it undermines their ability to trust girls. It's heartbreaking. A guy longs for a girl whom he can trust with his heart.

It has always been that way. In Bible days, when the Israelites defeated their enemies in battle, they would often bring home the plunder, the riches captured from the enemy. This was called spoil. It could consist of anything from gold, silver, jewels and garments, to cattle, sheep, camels, horses, etc. (Numbers 31:9; 2 Chronicles 20:25, KJV).

How the men must have enjoyed bringing those riches home to their wives! But can you imagine how crushed a guy felt who returned home from war to a wife who was disappointed because he didn't bring anything back for her? Surely he must have hoped she would be relieved, grateful and thrilled just that he returned safe! Proverbs 31:11 describes this longing. "The heart of her husband doth safely trust in her, so that he shall have no need of spoil" (KJV). Guys today have the same longing. *Will she love me without the "spoil"?*

Does She Care to Learn?

Guys don't expect girls to be perfect. When it comes to being good marriage material, guys are in the same boat as you. Becoming a good wife—or husband—is a learning process!

> When guys look at girls' homemaking skills, what the guys most want to know is, "Does she care to learn?"

Their questions about girls' domestic abilities are reasonable. But, let's face it, there's little chance a guy is going to quiz you on most of this stuff, point-blank. And they're not about to have you fill out a questionnaire before they ask you for a date! So we females need to work out these issues among ourselves.

While we're at it, let's pray that guys will learn what *they* need to! Manners, like homemaking skills, have nearly become a lost art. Because chivalry was rejected by zealous feminists, young men who know proper etiquette are now an endangered species. But there's hope!

A new generation of girls is rising up, young ladies who are releasing their princess within. And . . .

> Wherever there's a princess, there's sure to be a knight in shining armor on the way!

Trust me, that aroma wafting from your kitchen, of fresh homemade chocolate chip cookies, will lead him right to you.

Now, it wouldn't be fair to tell you all this without giving you such a recipe, so here's how to get that yummy chocolate chip cookies aroma in *your* kitchen.

IMPORTANT: Please **read the whole recipe before starting** so that . . .

. . . you have all needed ingredients.

. . . you combine ingredients in the proper order.

. . . you understand proper measuring techniques.

Chocolate Chip Cookies

1. Preheat oven to 375 degrees F.

2. Measure dry ingredients first. In a medium sized mixing bowl, combine:

   a. 1¾ cups all-purpose flour (Tip: When measuring flour, spoon it into your measuring cup. If you swoop the measuring cup through your container of flour, the flour will pack too densely. You'll have more flour than needed, and that can drastically affect the outcome of your cookies! After spooning flour into cup, level it off by scraping across the top of the cup with a straight edge, such as a knife.)

   b. 1 teaspoon salt (level with straight edge)

   c. ¾ teaspoon baking soda (level with straight edge) (Tip: Don't confuse this with baking powder. They are not the same.)

Mix dry ingredients well. Set aside.

3. In a separate mixing bowl, combine:

   a. ¾ cup vegetable shortening (Tip: Transfer shortening into your measuring cup using a spatula or spoon. Tap the cup firmly on the counter a few times to eliminate air pockets and help the shortening pack down. Level with straight edge.)

   b. 1¼ cups <u>light</u> <u>brown</u> sugar, packed (Tip: To measure brown sugar, firmly press it into measuring cup.)

   c. ¼ teaspoon butter flavoring (Tip: When measuring liquids into a measuring spoon, do this over a small container, rather than over your ingredients, so that if you spill, you won't have excess liquids in your batter.)

    d. 2 tablespoons milk

    e. 1 tablespoon vanilla

4. With an electric mixer, beat shortening, light brown sugar, butter flavoring, milk and vanilla until well blended. (Tip: Shut off machine and scrape bowl a couple times to make sure sides of bowl aren't collecting unmixed ingredients.)

5. Add to sticky ingredients (called a creamed mixture)

    a. 1 egg (Tip: When adding eggs to a recipe, break egg into a small container first. This prevents pieces of eggshell from falling into your batter. If a bit of shell falls into your small container, scoop it out with a larger piece of eggshell. Trying to do it with your finger or a spoon only makes that shell fragment flee.)

6. Add the dry ingredients to your creamed mixture with your electric mixer on low and beat just until blended.

7. Stir in:

    a. 1½ cups semisweet chocolate chips

8. Drop rounded tablespoonfuls of dough about 3 inches apart on an ungreased cookie sheet. (Tip: Placing the dough mounds—about the size of a small walnut—in rows, three across and four down, will fit a dozen cookies on a sheet.)

9. Bake 1 pan of cookies for 8 to 10 minutes. (Note: Ovens vary. I bake mine for 9 minutes.) (Tip: Most people prefer their cookies chewy. When you remove the pan from the oven, cookies will be light and may appear underbaked. Let cookies sit on pan for 2 to 3 minutes before removing onto paper toweling, or a cookie rack.) If you prefer crispier cookies, bake longer; try 11 minutes.

Recipe makes about 2½ dozen cookies.

Every hero wants a refuge where he can take off his armor. When a guy finds a girl who has strong homemaking skills, it says to him that she knows how to make such a place for her warrior. That can melt the heart of a guy and make him willing indeed to lay down his life for her as Christ laid down his life for the church he loved.

Oh, one more tip. Until you're married, keep some mystery about your cooking skills too. After all, not *every* guy deserves your best culinary delights!

Secret No. 12

Guys Have a Unique Relationship with Their Moms

What if I were to tell you that regardless of what guy captures your heart, and no matter how or where you meet him, there's already another woman in his life? This lady has major influence on him, and she's a female you can't ignore. It's true! And it's his mom. Yet if you're like most girls, when it comes to finding the guy of her dreams, the last thing a girl wants to consider is his mother. That's a huge mistake and it's a large part of how in-law problems start.

[
"In-law problems! Who's thinking about in-laws?
I don't even have a boyfriend!"
]

"I just met the cutest guy and he asked me out, but I'm sure not thinking about in-laws! All I'm thinking about is finding the right outfit and making sure I don't have a bad hair day!"

"I've never met my steady's parents."

"Well, I'm engaged, but it's no big deal. We'll be living miles from his family!"

See what I mean? When females dream about Prince Charming, their fantasies just don't tend to include the queen. But she's a very real part of the picture.

A guy's relationship with his mom begins even before he sees the light of day as a newborn. Nestled within her womb for approximately nine months, the first female voice he hears and the first female heartbeat he ever feels is that of his mother.

After the little male arrives in this world, he's still nestled close to his mama as she feeds him, changes his diapers and nurtures him. He grows, learns and develops under her watchful eye in the years that follow. By the time a girlfriend comes on the scene, many years have forged the link between mother and son. The young lady who doesn't understand this bond is headed for years of strife and heartache. The good news is it doesn't have to be that way! That's why this secret is so crucial.

Guys have a special relationship with their moms. Sometimes, it's very public. Like during a football game on TV. How many times have you seen a close-up of a sweaty, grinning player looking into the camera? What does he inevitably say? "Hi, Mom."

The list of distinguished men who give tribute to their mothers is long. Abraham Lincoln made a statement about his that is still quoted. "All that I am, or hope to be, I owe to my angel mother."

A few years ago, I had the privilege of hearing an account of the battle of Iwo Jima from a Marine veteran who was there. (This is a well-known conflict from World War II. People connect it with the famous photo of U.S. soldiers on a hill, raising the American flag.)

It tore at my heart to learn that most of the soldiers in that fight were teenagers. Then the retired lieutenant colonel said something else that to this day I cannot talk about without tears. He described how the wounded young men cried for their mothers as they lay suffering and dying. Was this a sign that those soldiers were weak? No. I believe it was a sacred revelation of the place that mothers hold in the hearts of sons.

We see another powerful portrayal of this holy bond when we look at Jesus' crucifixion. In his last moments of excruciating suffering and agony, Jesus too thought of his mother. He looked down at her from the cross and entrusted her into the care of his disciple John (John 19:25-27).

Jesus revered his mother. Since he is our example, we can conclude that it's perfectly natural for a man to have a place in his heart for his mother.

Not all guys grow up with a happy home life, but every guy's life is impacted by his mother in one way or another. Therefore, if you're in love with a guy, her presence or her mark will touch your life too.

The Importance of Family

The ideal time to consider your future in-laws is before you ever fall in love! Extended families play a much larger role in a marriage than most couples realize. And the way to avoid a lifetime of heartache is to take parents into consideration in all your relationships with guys.

In the old-fashioned days of courting, parents were extensively involved in an unfolding romance between their son and daughter. When a guy had his eyes on a certain girl . . .

In order to spend time with her, the young man had to first meet her parents and obtain permission from the dad to visit (court) her.

He then became acquainted with the young lady by spending time with her and her family.

The compatibility of a potential couple showed up almost before a young man paid his first visit. Generally, if the two families got along and approved of the relationship, the couple had a much greater chance of a happy marriage.

Those days of "front porch courting" were sweet, romantic and under the protective care of concerned parents. Now they seem archaic, if not laughable to most teens and their parents as well. Those old-fashioned methods of socializing and finding a mate have been replaced with what we now call dating.

Today, the "wow" factor between a girl and guy still begins in basically the same places—school, church, work, social events—and for the same fun reasons. But parents often aren't as involved as they used to be. This might be because they're busy, because the family is broken or because the girl and guy aren't communicating with their parents. A young couple might even go steady without their moms and dads knowing. The more common time for their folks to be included in the picture is when a couple decides to marry. But by that time, the couple has already set themselves up for a potential lifetime of problems.

Today's divorce rates are a sad indicator that this new method of finding a mate isn't all that great. (I know it's not new to you, but compared to historical traditions which involved parents, independent dating is a very recent trend.)

Though we don't need to go back to the days of arranged marriages (OK, that's exaggerating), there is still something that girls can do to up the odds in their favor for wedded bliss. That is to once again begin acknowledging the importance of family.

Families are meant to be a built-in support system. The wisdom and counsel of parents, the encouragement of siblings and the joy of extended family all play a huge role in the success of a marriage. Independent dating often excludes this support system. If you start a relationship without inviting your parents' involvement, and without considering a guy's parents, you're building on a severely weakened foundation.

There's No Way Around It

Families have an influence from which you cannot escape! That's a major reason for taking a look at them before you fall in love.

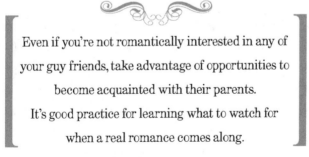

Even if you're not romantically interested in any of your guy friends, take advantage of opportunities to become acquainted with their parents.
It's good practice for learning what to watch for when a real romance comes along.

And it's a great chance to try your skills at relating with a guy's mom in a setting that feels less threatening. Make it your goal to scope out guys' parents well before you give your heart away. What you learn can help you decide whether or not you want to go further into a friendship.

Regardless of the depth of your relationship with a guy, here are some things to watch for.

• **Observe how a guy treats his mother.** Is he polite, kind, thoughtful, helpful, loving? His actions are clues on how he will treat the next important lady in his life—his wife! Will you want to be treated the way he treats his mother?

• **Notice how she relates to him.** Does she listen to him? Is she friendly, encouraging? Everyone knows some mothers can be domineering or possessive. That's why you need to take family characteristics into consideration now. If a guy has a controlling mother, you will feel her influence too. However unwanted, her involvement will be something that you have to deal with if you fall in love with and marry this guy.

[Family dynamics don't evaporate at the altar.]

Also, there may be issues in this young man's life that you might want to think about. Are you sure you want a husband who is used to being bossed around or manipulated by his mother? If she's overbearing, your guy could have difficulty being a leader for his own family. That doesn't mean a girl must rule out as a potential husband every guy who comes from these circumstances. But you might have challenges.

This is where your influence can be a blessing—provided you're not an overbearing girlfriend! The guy who has a bossy mother won't fare well with a nagging fiancée. You won't get along well either. When a possessive wife and a controlling mother confront each other, it's like a hot, humid air mass meeting with a cold, dry front. The resulting tornado destroys everything in its path!

But your meek and quiet spirit and lots of prayer can accomplish much. Don't strive with his mom but gently help your guy believe in himself. You can have positive influence if you treat him with respect and honor and encourage him to take his role as leader. I doubt there's a guy on earth who doesn't love to hear, "I believe in you." (Think how much the Lord loves to hear this!) Remember though, that his mother will be in the picture too. In relating to her, a sense of humor might work wonders, even if it's only in your own thoughts that you lighten up.

• **Pay attention to a guy's interaction with his siblings.** Does he build them up? Is he kind, supportive, protective?

• **Note how a guy's parents relate with each other.** They are modeling a marriage and your guy friend is learning from them. Whether he realizes it or not, he's taking cues from their interaction, for good or bad. Is his mother respectful and submissive to his father? How does his dad treat his mom? Do they seem close?

What about his dad? Does he lead the family or stay in the background while mom runs the show? Is he kind? Friendly? Is he a hard worker?

• **Take note of your own parents' relationship as well**. Whether you realize it or not, you are learning from them. You and your future husband will both carry certain expectations into your marriage without realizing it.

Stepping Heavenward, a fiction book written in the 1800s by Miss E. Prentiss, gives a great example of this. Presented in diary form, the heroine discloses problems that crop up with her husband after their marriage. She simply can't understand the source of their conflict until she confides in her sister-in-law. She learns that in her husband's family, the women treated the men as kings. They made sure the menfolk were not only taken care of but also doted on.

In the heroine's family, however, the women were on the receiving end of the pampering! Papa took great care to cover them with kindness and to meet their every need. She grew up with no doubt that she was precious!

When that indulged man and that coddled lady were wed, each of them went into the marriage expecting to be the star who received special treatment. Even though they truly loved each other, he couldn't understand why she wasn't always fawning over him and she didn't understand why he showed so little concern for her welfare.

Expectations for marriage and family life come from what you observe between your parents and the families around you and from what you experience while growing up. Without realizing it, you can harbor expectations of your husband and then be disillusioned because he's not fulfilling them. Your husband may not have a clue about what you're thinking. Likewise, your hubby might be puzzled when you're not meeting his expectations. Observing a guy's family gives you inside info in plenty of time to learn their ways and make informed decisions.

• **Note how your guy friend gets along with his father.** If he isn't respectful and obedient to his dad, is he likely to be respectful to other authority figures, like a boss or the Lord? Would he make a good spiritual leader for your family? By his conduct with his parents now, the guy is sowing into the future of his own family. If he can't relate to his mother and dad properly, how will he be able to teach your children to respect you as parents?

There will be numerous clues as to whether or not in-law harmony is possible. Watch for them. Pray for discernment. You'll be able to see well before you give your heart away what lies ahead if you become part of that family.

Marriage is not just a two-person contract. Each of you is marrying into the other's family. Pay attention if problems with potential in-laws appear because, left untended, those problems will get worse, not better, after the wedding.

Wives-to-be tend to think, *As soon as we're man and wife, I've got him and we can finally start our own life.* In one sense, that's true. But you will never be able to sever your husband from his family. It's impossible to totally cut off their influence.

> Your potential husband is a composite of his parents and ancestors. No single ceremony can separate him from all of that.

To deny your fiancé's family is to deny a major part of his identity—and half the identity of your future children! His parents are not just your possible in-laws, they could be your children's grandparents. Will they make the kind of grandmother and grandfather you want for them?

Realize that your guy's family is going to have an affect on you. This isn't something that you can escape from or wish away. The connection is there. Ask anyone who has been married for a while if in-laws play a part in that person's marriage. Please don't misunderstand; I am definitely not saying that in-laws are awful people! But no matter what they are like, their mark on your lives will be significant. To ignore this is not only unfair to the guy in your life but also to his family, and certainly to you.

If you find yourself wanting to pull your boyfriend away from his family, maybe you need to examine your heart. Why would you want to do that? God is a Redeemer. All of his purposes are redemptive (Psalm 130:7). God is not bringing the two of you together so that you may separate a guy from his family. It's the exact opposite! God is giving you an awesome *ministry* and *message* to promote wholeness within his family!

"This is from God, who reconciled us to himself through Christ and gave us the ministry of reconciliation . . . and he has committed to us the message of reconciliation" (2 Corinthians 5:18, 19).

You are God's ambassador to a guy's family for the Lord's redemptive purposes. What a precious privilege!

So acknowledging the importance of extended family is major! Are there other things a girl can do to move toward harmony with my boyfriend's family, especially his mom?

That's the attitude you want, and the answer to your question is YES! Following are some tips to help you be a young lady whom any mom would love to have for a daughter-in-law. But before we look at them, let's do a little daydreaming . . . into your happily ever after.

A Dream About You

Veiled and arrayed in a gown of lily white, you wait, breathless, for the music to signal your walk down the aisle. At the altar, with his eyes locked in your direction, stands the man of your dreams. Who would ever believe two people could love each other so much. But it's true. And this time it's you!

The scene fades momentarily and then refocuses.

This time your gown is pale green. Hospital garb. And your whole body is trembling. You lift your head to gaze at the squalling miracle just placed on your belly, and you cradle him in your arms. Who would ever believe a woman could love another guy so much. But it's true. And this time it's you.

Again the scene dissolves. It comes back to reveal a room softly illuminated by a night-light.

You're wearing a gown again. This time it's a pink print with small rosebuds. And it's flannel. You shuffle over to the bunk bed, reach out and touch his brow. The fever has broken. You sink down on the chair in the corner and release silent tears of relief. Who would ever believe a son could command such a vigilance of love. But it's true. And this time it's you.

The picture closes once more, and then snaps back, bright and clear.

He's wearing a gown of royal blue; a matching blue and silver tassel dangles from the cap. School colors. He strides across the platform, shakes hands with dignitaries and descends the steps, diploma in hand. At the reception, joy radiates from his face as he bounds in your direction for a mother-son hug. But he never makes it. A young lady intersects his path and grabs his hand. Who would ever believe two women could love the same guy so much. But it's true. And this time . . . she takes him away . . . from you.

Can you feel my gentle nudge? It was only a daydream. An imaginary visit into the heart of a mother, though someday it could very well be you. With this vision still fresh, I hope the following tips will seem more reasonable and make more sense.

[
"Blessed are the peacemakers: for they shall be called the children of God" (Matthew 5:9, KJV).
]

A Peaceful Girlfriend, Fiancée or Daughter-in-law . . .

• **Will be friendly toward her guy's mom.** She will respect his mother's present place of importance in his life. Take a look back at Secret No. 7. We've finally come to that missing point from the list of reasons to hesitate before phoning a guy! *If you phone a guy, especially when he's in middle school or early high school, he might be uncomfortable talking with you because of house rules.*

Not all mothers (and dads) feel that it's appropriate for girls to phone their sons. Others are fine with it but not past a certain time of night. Some moms flex according to the circumstances. Rules will vary according to the family. If these moms bug you, it might be a sign that you're already off to a bad start in relating with a future mother-in-law. There's an extremely important reason to rethink your attitude, and I'll tell you about it before the end of this chapter.

• **Will not try to isolate her husband from his parents, siblings and family.** Isolation may seem to work for a while but sooner or later—and it could take years—the family ties will surface. We are who we are, forever. There's no question that God can change him, but your guy is always going to have his original earthly foundations.

In Secret No. 8, I gave you a list of benefits of not being possessive of your boyfriend. One point said: "Not being possessive is good practice for issues that will crop up later. Hint: It has to do with other key people in your life." Well, in-law ties are those other issues! Your guy's parents and siblings are those other key people! If you've practiced sharing your boyfriend with his friends, I know you won't have trouble sharing your husband with his family!

• **Will not make her husband have to choose between his mom and her.** If you compete for your husband's exclusive affection, you're saying he must make a choice to stop loving one of you. That is selfish and unloving. If you do that, you are not loving *him*. Why should he have to choose? A mother and a wife are by no means in the same category. You and your mother-in-law have different roles.

> Do you want to be your husband's mother,
> or do you want to be his wife?

Besides, a guy who is so wonderful that you would choose to marry him must surely have a heart big enough to love his wife, his mom, his sisters, brothers and everyone else God trusts to his care—all without conflict!

• **Will refuse to be in competition with her mother-in-law.** This is where girls often make a mistake. A girl looks at her guy's mom and automatically thinks that his mother is the enemy and that she has to compete with the mother-in-law for his devotion.

Oh, no! Instead, make her your ally! Attitude is so important here. Remember, it was his mother (and dad) who raised him to become the super guy that you want to marry! Doesn't it make sense that she would have marvelous resources you could tap into and learn from? She can be a valuable asset to you.

Look at your mother-in-law as a treasure! Hey, she raised him; she must have tons of secrets to his heart . . . what he likes and doesn't like! Who better than her to share tidbits to give you an edge on being a blessing to this guy?

Someday, the fiancée of one of my sons is going to hear from me how much he likes back rubs (and has since he was an infant)! These are the kind of secrets you want to pull out of your mother-in-law. Of course that means you have to be teachable. She can't share information with you if you're not open to her. But . . .

[
What fun it is when a mom and daughter-in-law
put their heads together to bless the same guy!
]

As newlyweds, my husband Kevin and I lived in Canada and his mother lived in Arizona. She was a really good cook. She made the best cinnamon and sticky rolls! And her meat loaf, Spanish rice and coleslaw were all dishes that my husband loved. I knew this because he told me. Then an opportunity opened for us to visit her.

All that could have been intimidating for a new wife. But instead of jealousy driving a wedge between us, my mother-in-law and I bonded in her kitchen. She taught me all those recipes! We had so much fun together. She enjoyed teaching, I loved learning and everyone benefited—

especially Kevin!

When it comes to competing with your in-laws, here's something else to consider. Your guy's mom has known him longer than you have. Think about it. You will have to be married for as many years as his age when he marries you before you'll know your husband as long as his parents and family have known him. For example, if your fiancé is twenty-three when you marry, you will need to be married nearly twenty-three years before you will know him as long as his parents have. Don't waste time trying to compete with that!

• **Will be a support to her husband, concerning his family.** It's a myth that in-laws can't be enjoyed. There's no need for competition and jealousy. Your guy chose *you*, didn't he? Relax. Encourage him to stay close with his mother, father, brothers and sisters!

> Don't feel threatened when your guy and his mom have a mother-son moment. Be thankful that he reveres his mother.

The same goes for his sister. The guy who praises his mom's cooking and who adores his sister is a special guy! Don't spoil his joy. Take delight in those ladies *with* him!

Let him spend time with his family . . . even without you! He doesn't stop being a son or a brother when he becomes a husband. Encourage him to keep his family ties strong. Guys will always need breathing room! Give it to him with your blessing.

Have you noticed there hasn't been much said about fathers-in-law?

That's because the majority of in-law problems stem from the women. Whether it's mother-in-law vs. daughter-in-law or wife vs. sister-in-law, the strife usually develops among the females. I'm not saying that men are never a problem, but it's more commonly the women. And in this secret we're looking at guys and their moms.

Don't Break the Law!

Remember a bit ago when I said there's an important reason to re-think your attitude toward guys' moms, even while you're too young for marriage? We've arrived at that reason!

God has set up certain laws in the universe which apply to everyone, such as the law of gravity. We all know this law works whether or not we believe in God, right? What goes up must come down. One can't defy the law of gravity without paying the consequences.

Another of God's irrefutable precepts is the law of sowing and reaping. People who don't acknowledge God often phrase it a bit differently. They say, "What goes around comes around." Nearly everyone has a clear understanding that actions and treatment tend to circle back to a person. But the law of sowing and reaping is easier to forget because we don't always see the consequences right away.

Whatever your age, when it comes to relationships, the law of sowing and reaping is critical because you will fill several roles throughout life. Right now, you're already a daughter. Maybe you're also a sister. Beyond that, you have the potential to be a wife, which will also make you a daughter-in-law! And you may become a mother, which means that someday you could become a mother-in-law! This is a lot of different roles for a girl in one lifetime, isn't it? That's why the law of sowing and reaping is so crucial.

> If you isolate your boyfriend or disrespect a guy's
> mom now, think of the harvest you have to look
> forward to when you are a mother! Being on the
> receiving end is not a nice thought, is it?

The wife who separates her husband from his mother, dad, brothers or sisters has that isolation to look forward to at some point in time. A selfish daughter-in-law sets herself up for a miserable future as a mother-in-law. Females may attempt to cut off their guys from relatives—but what are they doing? They're sowing seeds for an unhappy future!

Regardless of your role now, what kind of harvest do you want? If you wish to remain close with your children when they're grown, and you want a warm and joyful relationship with their spouses, the time to sow seed for that loving environment is now! Jesus said, "So in everything, do to others what you would have them do to you" (Matthew 7:12).

There's no guarantee that you're going to have an ideal situation where your heart is perfect, your husband's heart is perfect, your mother-in-law's heart is perfect and everything is just nice. But when things aren't so smooth, there are still things you can do to promote goodwill. You want your mother-in-law to know that you're not trying to take her son away, don't you?

With what we now know about guys and their moms, let's go back to that daydream and replay the last scene. . . .

He's wearing a gown of royal blue; a matching blue and silver tassel dangles from the cap. School colors. He strides across the platform, shakes hands with dignitaries and descends the steps, diploma in hand. At the reception, joy radiates from his face as he bounds in your direction for a mother-son hug. But he doesn't make it. A young lady intersects his path and grabs his hand. Who would ever believe two women could love the same guy so much. But it's true. And this time . . . she beams in your direction while together they bound . . . toward you.

It's so much more pleasant to be generous in relationships. Here are a few more ideas for interacting with extended family in a way that can make time spent with them positive.

- Gratitude is always appropriate. Thank your guy's mother for her example and/or for anything she teaches you.
- Thank her for giving birth to your guy.
- Thank her for raising him and pouring herself into his life.
- Befriend his sister. He won't love you less if he admires her. She's not out to steal your hubby.
- Support and encourage your guy's relationship with his parents and siblings. I'm glad to see my husband visit his family as often as possible, even when I can't go along. I pray he'll always be close with his siblings. This strengthens his family and ours as well. It's good seed!
- Ask specifically for the blessing of your mother-and-father-in-law.

So much of this issue about in-laws is attitude.

> Fear, jealousy and competition are common among families, but we don't have to accept those joy stealers. It's possible to have the harmony for which Jesus prayed . . .

and to change the whole view of what in-law relationships are about (John 17:20-23).

As a future wife and daughter-in-law, you play a key role in your own happiness as well as your husband's. Instead of dividing your families, you can multiply the joy. And it's well worth the effort!

Conclusion

Y ou have just taken a backstage tour inside the hearts and minds of guys. In the process, you discovered a ton of secrets that guys want you to know . . . and maybe a few they'd rather you *didn't* find out! But that's OK. When it comes to having great relationships with guys, you deserve as much inside info as possible!

Did we uncover absolutely everything? Definitely not! There are things I was forbidden to disclose! Isn't that fun?

Guys are individuals. Each one has his own unique secrets. To get the rest of the scoop about *your* guy, there's still another source—our heavenly Father! That's right! He is the master revealer of secrets (Daniel 2:22, 28, 29, KJV)! He knows the deep and hidden things about all the guys in your life because he created them. When you're really stumped, you can go directly to him! And I hope you will.

I pray that this book has launched you on a great adventure and that learning these secrets and putting them into practice will bring great rewards!

True Stories of Teens on a Sacred Journey

ENCOUNTERSWITHGOD

10 poetic expressions and 52 relevant issue-oriented stories written by teens for teens.

Meeting teens' needs at various places in their spiritual journey

Encounters with God, 23354

Order your copy now by calling 1-800-543-1353 or by visiting your local Christian bookstore.

Compiled by Kelly Carr

Dream.

Draw.

Reflect.

sanctuary
a journal to download my ideas,
remember experiences,
draw and dream . . .

02957

canvas
a journal to download my ideas,
remember experiences,
draw and dream . . .

02956

sacrifice
a journal to download my ideas,
remember experiences,
draw and dream . . .

02958

BEYOND

a journal

COMPILED BY LYNN LUSET PRATT
AUTHOR OF DEVOTIONS BY DEAD PEOPLE

02900

*spiral-bound
art journals
for you to
take reflective
refuge from
the world and
express what
God is doing in
your life.*

ref·uge \ˈre-fyüj \
shelter or protection from danger or distress

"My salvation and my honor come from God alone.
He is my refuge, a rock where no enemy can reach me.
O my people, trust in him at all times.
Pour out your heart to him,
for God is our refuge."
—Psalm 62: 7, 8, NLT

In the Old Testament God provided six "cities of refuge" where a person could seek safe haven from vengeance. These cities were places of protection. Today refuge™ will provide you the safe haven you need to grow in your relationship with God.

 www.rfgbooks.com